STORM THE GATES

Storm the Gates

Provoking the Church to Fulfill God's Mission

NATHAN COOK

Storm the Gates: Provoking the Church to Fulfill God's Mission

Published by Bridgetown Ventures
P.O. Box 22115
Memphis, TN 38122
www.bridgetownventures.org

Library of Congress Control Number: 2020903955

ISBN: 978-1-7346-9261-7

Cover design: Jason Stevens

To my wife Kim and our three children Caleb, Grace, and Ella for seeking Jesus and his kingdom with faith and perseverance.

"Let us not glide through this world and then slip quietly into heaven, without having blown the trumpet loud and long for our redeemer, Jesus Christ. Let us see to it that the devil will hold a thanksgiving service in Hell when he gets the news of our departure from the field of battle."

C.T. Studd

CONTENTS

INTRODUCTION 1

1 GOD'S VISION FOR THE CHURCH 9

2 YOU ARE CALLED 25

3 PRAY FOR GOD'S KINGDOM 45

4 HOW TO OBEY GOD 59

5 LIVE BY FAITH AND NOT BY FEAR 73

6 SEEK SHALOM 85

7 HONOR GOD WITH YOUR TITHE 101

8 LOVE YOUR NEIGHBOR 115

9 CULTIVATE A SPIRIT OF GENEROSITY 127

10 FORGIVENESS: THE POWER OF THE GOSPEL 137

11 GO AND BEAR FRUIT 149

BRIDGETOWN 165

INTRODUCTION

After I graduated from college, I had the opportunity to lead a mission trip to Russia. My church in Memphis had started a new church in Russia, two years before our trip. Our team was going to conduct outreach to the youth in their city. The new church arranged to host a week-long event at a former Communist indoctrination camp.

The camp was similar in appearance to a Boy Scout camp. There were cabins with bunk beds, a large kitchen and a common dining area. There were also some distinctly Russian elements. In the afternoons, men would gather at the *banya* to take a sauna and to drink hot tea.

It was five years after the Soviet Union had dissolved. New expressions of Christian freedom were emerging in the former Communist states, but almost all the Russian youth who attended our camp identified as atheists. They arrived at the camp eager to socialize with their American counterparts.

Our team of youth and adult leaders led the activities for the week. We shared the gospel through art, drama, sporting events, and Bible studies. It was the first cross-cultural experience for many of the people on our team.

Matt was one of the teenagers on our team. He struggled throughout the trip. He thought the food was awful. He complained of uncomfortable accommodations and made unreasonable requests from our hosts. His behavior embarrassed me, and he even became a distraction for our team. At one point, I considered purchasing a plane ticket to send him home early.

Near the end of our trip, Matt played the role of Jesus in a dramatization of the crucifixion. His performance was brilliant. Two-thirds of the youth made a profession of faith at the conclusion of Matt's performance. These young Russian Christians became a new generation of leaders in their churches.

It was the most successful mission trip I've led, and it taught me several lessons that I still draw on to this day. When I stopped focusing on Matt's immaturity, I realized he was a model of Christian faithfulness. He obeyed Jesus' teaching to make disciples of all nations despite his frustrations with the culture. He accepted risks that outsized his young Christian faith. He traveled to a foreign land that was still hostile to Christianity. He endured discomfort so others would be comforted by the gospel. He used his gift of acting to draw others to Christ.

Despite his immaturity, God used Matt as a vessel for his grace. Through Matt's example, I came to understand that our shortcomings actually help others to see the grace of God more clearly. Vulnerability is a gift from God. Allowing others to see our flaws highlights God's goodness and his grace at work within us. God doesn't expect perfection from us. He is looking for imperfect people who are willing to surrender their agendas for his own.

Throughout this book, I share how God has worked through my own weaknesses. God's mission has always been carried out by broken people. Thus, every follower of Jesus has the potential to impact the world for Christ. The key to our success lies in our willingness to surrender to the Holy Spirit, allowing God to work through our weaknesses.

Surrendering to Jesus

When I was twelve years old, I made a decision to follow Jesus at a youth event sponsored by my church. As the guest preacher spoke about God's holiness and our sinfulness, I felt convicted. I was broken by my sinfulness and was in awe of God's grandeur. Tears flowed relentlessly. A youth counselor brought me to the preacher so we could pray together. I confessed every sin I could remember, begging for God's forgiveness. As I prayed, I experienced a growing sense of dread that finally expressed itself in a single thought: *my life doesn't belong to me anymore.*

Surrendering to God was a fearful endeavor for me. Following Jesus meant I was losing control of determining my own future. I wanted forgiveness for my sins and the peace God would provide, but I didn't want to give up control of my life in the process.

Men in our church played a pivotal role in helping me learn how to surrender my life to Jesus. Over the next couple of years, youth leaders in my church helped me to read and to understand the Bible. We discussed passages of scripture together and thought of ways to put Jesus' teachings into practice.

My youth minister started a ministry called Service Over Self (SOS) to teach teenagers how to love their neighbors. SOS still exists today as an urban home repair camp. Youth volunteer during the spring and summer to fix homes for people living in poverty. Volunteering with SOS opened my eyes to racial and class inequities in our city. It gave me an opportunity to build meaningful relationships across class barriers.

SOS planted a vision in me for urban ministry that would grow during my time at Asbury Seminary. One of my professors introduced me to John Perkins and the Christian Community Development Association (CCDA). John was a Christian civil rights leader who preached on the importance of relocation and of living among the poor while working toward class and racial reconciliation. I joined a small group of seminarians who wanted to put John's teaching into practice.

Eight of us moved into three different houses in downtown Lexington, KY. We started a church among the homeless. On Saturday mornings, my roommates and I would host breakfast for our neighbors in our home. On two different occasions, we invited homeless men to live with us until they could get back on their feet. The concept of the church began to change for me. I stopped seeing the church as a *place* where Christians gathered for worship. I started seeing the church as a group of *people* who carried out God's mission in the world together.

Months before graduating from seminary, I started feeling prompted to move back to Memphis. I felt led to seek the welfare of the city by pursuing justice for the poor. I had a recurring dream of walking around the park where SOS hosted picnics for its volunteers and homeowners. I felt like God was calling me to move into the park's surrounding neighborhood and to raise my family there.

I wasn't married at the time. I couldn't imagine that any woman in her right mind would move into an inner-city community with me. My fears started getting the best of me. I imagined that following Jesus into the inner city would lead to a life of celibacy. I got up the courage to talk to my girlfriend, Kim, about my commitment to relocation. I told her about my dreams and that I was planning to move to an inner-city neighborhood one day. I wanted to continue dating, but I felt like Kim needed to know that relocating to an urban neighborhood was a non-negotiable for me.

As we talked, Kim shared a couple of non-negotiables of her own. As a ten-year-old girl, God had given her a heart for adoption. "If you can't imagine raising several adopted children one day," she suggested, "we should probably stop dating now." On top of that, Kim had been a part of a vibrant campus ministry in college that had sent over seventy people to serve as missionaries overseas. She had always envisioned herself equipping people to serve as missionaries abroad.

Instead of pushing us apart, our conversation solidified our relationship. We trusted each other with the deepest longings of our hearts. Our desires to serve God were met with encouragement and affirmation from each other. Although we didn't know how God would weave these seemingly disparate ministries together, we trusted God to work it out in time. Kim and I married the following year. We moved into Binghampton, an urban neighborhood in Memphis, six months after our wedding.

Understanding God's Mission

When we arrived in Memphis, we found other people who had a similar vision for relocation. A young man named David moved into Binghampton to teach youth about the Bible. A married couple, both doctors, moved into the neighborhood to be closer to their patients. A young couple with SOS relocated to integrate with the community they served. God was drawing together a network of people who had a common desire to live among the poor.

Soon, we were living together, working together, and worshiping God together. We decided to form a church together that met weekly in our home. As our group grew, we formed new house churches. New home groups eventually spread to several different urban neighborhoods throughout our city.

In time, we learned that urban ministry was a breeding ground for missionaries. The same skills needed to thrive overseas could be acquired in our neighborhoods. Members of our house churches learned to overcome fear and cross-cultural barriers with faith and to love the marginalized.

We equipped house church leaders to share the gospel with their neighbors and to lead small group discussions about the Bible. With the help of a seasoned missionary, members of our house churches relocated to North Africa and the Middle East to start new churches. God was beginning to weave Kim's and my desires together. In time, all three strands of ministry that Kim and I discussed in seminary found expression through our church.

In 2005, we adopted our first child. In 2009, we adopted our second. Kim became involved with a network of moms in our city who were learning how to heal trauma in adopted children. Soon, others in our church were pursuing adoption and foster care as well. Kim began to mentor young moms through the process of adoption. Over the years, more than 25 families from our network of house churches adopted or fostered children.

Our desire for ministry was grounded in God's word. We desired to defend the rights of the poor and needy (Proverbs 31:9), to visit the fatherless in their distress (James 1:27), and to make disciples of all nations (Matthew 28:18-20). God transformed these desires into the core values of our church.

Once a month, our house churches gathered together for a corporate worship service. At one of those gatherings, Eric gave an analogy that finally put into words what we were feeling in our hearts. Eric was an elder in our church and the executive director of SOS. He consolidated our thoughts about ministry into a single image that communicated our vision for the church.

Eric said our service to God is like a sai. A sai is a traditional martial arts weapon. It has one long central blade with two shorter prongs that project upward from either side of its handle. Eric said our main purpose in life is to glorify God. God's glory is the long central blade of the sai. Two ways we can glorify God are by caring for the poor and taking the gospel to nations. The needs of the poor and the nations are the two smaller prongs of a sai.

When we obey God's word to care for the poor, and when we take the gospel to the nations, we are like a martial artist taking ground for God's kingdom. Satan's plans are rebuffed, and God is glorified. Some years later, I took a position with a Christian residency program. I trained doctors to work among the poor and to serve as missionaries overseas. We further simplified Eric's message to encourage the young physicians we trained. To remind themselves to forgo the comforts of the world in favor of sacrificial service to Jesus, our young physicians sewed patches on their scrubs with the motto, "To the Need, To the Nations, For the King!"

Provoking Obedience

The Christian author and apologist C.S. Lewis once wrote, "Enemy-occupied territory—that is what this world is. Christianity is the story of how the rightful king has landed...and is calling us all to take part in a great campaign of sabotage" (*Mere Christianity*, 46). Kim and I have counseled hundreds of young men and women who were discontent with the status quo. They realized that they were living in enemy-occupied territory. They were tempted to pursue a life of luxury, but they found those desires to be unsatisfying. They were ready to break with the prevailing culture and wanted to know how to discern God's will for their lives. They wanted to know how to become saboteurs, how to disrupt the kingdom of the world and take ground for King Jesus.

I am grateful to the men in my church who taught me how to obey Jesus by caring for the needs of others. They provided me with tangible examples of how to put the teachings of the Bible into practice. They helped me find an alternative to the American Dream.

American culture pushes us to seek comfort and pursue our own individual agendas. I wrote this book to persuade you to fulfill God's mission for the church and to help the poor while making disciples of all nations. Biblical faith is deeper and more rewarding than what cultural Christianity offers us. You have permission to abandon the American Dream to pursue a life less ordinary—a life directed "To the Need, To the Nations, For the King!"

The first two chapters of this book layout a framework for understanding our part in God's mission. God has set us apart from the world to confront the powers of Hell. We advance God's mission in the world through faith, obedience, and personal sacrifice. These first two chapters will help you to take a more active stance in pursuing God's mission. The last nine chapters contain lessons on how to express the values of God's kingdom in the world today. They will help you to love the poor and to make disciples of all nations.

My wife had a friend in college who prayed for people to be ruined for the ordinary so they might explore the deep riches of God's kingdom. It is my sincere hope that as you read this book, you will be ruined for the ordinary. I promise, if you spend time reflecting on the passages of scripture highlighted, new desires will be born in you. You will want to increase your dependence on Jesus to serve those who are in need of Christ's love. You will realize that God doesn't work through superheroes. He works through ordinary people like you and me. If you take Him at his word, trusting Jesus to work through you, you might find yourself storming the gates of Hell, loosening bonds of injustice by helping others to find freedom in Christ.

CHAPTER 1

GOD'S VISION FOR THE CHURCH

"And I tell you, you are Peter, and on this rock, I will build my church, and the gates of hell shall not prevail against it."
Matthew 16:18

Genocide was taking place in the Darfur region of Sudan when I was invited to build a rudimentary clinic for those suffering from the conflict. I had no construction skills myself, but a young engineer from our church named Eddie, and two very capable carpenters from SOS, had agreed to help. The clinic would be a single-room shelter, serving as a base of operation for short-term medical teams arriving in the months that followed.

My decision to lead the team was made in haste. Our partners overseas said there was a brief window of opportunity to get a team on the ground. There was a real openness to the gospel in the area. The Fur people were hurting spiritually and physically. If we were going, we needed to go now.

My wife, Kim, and I both grew in anxiety as the day of my departure drew near. Fearfulness was growing in our hearts, and our minds were filled with doubt. I started looking for excuses not to go. I did not have the money I needed for the flight to Sudan. Kim and I prayed for clarity of heart and mind. She threw out a fleece: "God, if you want Nathan to go on this trip, provide for our financial needs." The next day, we received an unsolicited check in the mail for $2,000. I was going to Darfur.

When our team arrived in Khartoum, we were placed under a travel ban. We were not allowed to leave the city. Instead of building a clinic, we spent our days encouraging our host and visiting with various ministry leaders. We waited for the travel ban to be lifted. It never was. Our plan to build a clinic never materialized. Our hope of sharing the gospel with the Fur people would have to wait. We returned home feeling deflated.

A year later, Eddie returned with his family to work with a mission team in Darfur. He had spent a couple of years there before the Sudanese government forced them to leave. Several years later, he returned to the mission field with his family to plant churches in a remote region of the world. Eddie faced new discouragements and setbacks, but again, he persevered in faith.

Today, we receive reports from his team of how God's kingdom is growing. People are coming to faith in Jesus. Our short-term trip had felt like a failure, but God used it to plant a vision for his kingdom in the heart of my friend. Through faith and perseverance, new expressions of God's kingdom are emerging at the very ends of the Earth.

Called to Confront Evil

It is easy to get discouraged when thinking about the condition of the world today. You don't have to travel to Darfur to experience racism, violence, and oppression. There is evidence of sin and brokenness all around us. Given our circumstances, we face a real temptation to retreat from the world. To create an enclave of comfort and security. To disengage from the problems that surround us. But Jesus didn't run from the problems of the world; he confronted them at their source, and he commissioned his church to do the same.

In Matthew 16:18, Jesus gave his disciples a new revelation about the church. Jesus said, "And I tell you, you are Peter, and on this rock, I will build my church, and the gates of Hell will not prevail against it." For the past twenty years, I have used this verse to help people reconsider God's purpose for his church. Many of my students interpret this verse to mean God will protect us from the attack of Satan and his minions.

But in the scripture passage, the forces of Hell are not attacking the church. The gates of Hell are not an offensive weapon. I've never seen a movie where one person attacked another person with a gate. A gun, yes. Bows and arrows, tanks and planes, of course. But a gate, never. Hell is not attacking the church with its gates.

In Jesus' day, every major city had a wall built around it. The wall was built to keep the city's inhabitants safe during times of war. The only way into or out of the city was through the city gates. When a foreign power threatened to attack, the city gates would be barricaded to keep the enemy at bay.

In Matthew 16:18, Jesus is using a walled city as a metaphor for Hell. Hell has blockaded its gates to keep the church at a safe distance, hoping to hold onto those it has taken captive. But Jesus has arrived on the scene as the rightful king, and he is taking back his kingdom. The forces of Hell cannot stop him. The forces of Hell are on the defensive, not the church.

Jesus calls his church to storm the gates of Hell. Like a general sending his troops to lay siege to a city, Jesus sent the church to batter down Hell's defenses. As the church proclaimed the gospel of Jesus Christ, those within Hell's confines were liberated. Their sins were forgiven. Their debts were paid. They were no longer under the dominion of the evil one. The captives who heard the good news and accepted it with faith were set free. Hell lost ground as the Kingdom of God advanced.

When Jesus said, "The gates of Hell will not prevail against the church," he promised that the church would be victorious. It would accomplish Jesus' mission to make disciples of all nations. It would teach people to obey all that Christ commanded. As we put Jesus' teachings into practice, the church will be an agent of change in the world. The forces of Hell cannot stop it.

The New Testament develops the theme of the church overthrowing the dominion of the evil one. In Matthew chapters 8-9, Jesus went from town to town, releasing people from spiritual bondage by healing the sick and casting out demons. Metaphorically speaking, Jesus was attacking the gates of Hell, freeing those who were in bondage to Satan.

In Matthew 10:1, Jesus gave his disciples the authority to deliver people from spiritual captivity. "And he called to him his twelve disciples and gave them authority over unclean spirits, to cast them out, and to heal every disease and every affliction." Moments later, Jesus sent the disciples on a missionary journey instructing them to "heal the sick, raise the dead, cleanse lepers, and cast out demons" (Matthew 10:8). The people of God were empowered to confront the forces of Hell. Those who suffered from spiritual bondage were set free by the grace of God expressed through the ministry of the disciples.

The conflict between the church and the dominion of Hell continued throughout the New Testament. The kingdom of God advanced as the church fulfilled its mission. In the book of Acts, Paul and Silas cast a demon out of a slave girl who was being exploited as a fortune teller. The girl was set free from the dominion of darkness. The evil spirit that resided in her was removed by the power of Christ through the ministry of Paul and Silas. Hell lost another captive and the kingdom of God grew. The slave girl's master was incensed. He could no longer exploit the girl for his financial gain. His source of revenue was lost. The resources at Hell's disposal dried up. Hell's defenses crumbled. Its mission to hold God's Kingdom at bay was threatened.

As Paul and Silas continued their ministry in Ephesus, the forces of Hell began to resist their advancement. When Paul preached the gospel, many stopped practicing magic and worshiping idols. As a sign of their repentance, the Ephesians burned their magic books. Idol makers, feeling that their way of life was under attack, stirred up a riot to oppose Paul and his ministry.

The Ephesians' cultural identity and economic prosperity were tied to the worship of Artemis, a Greek goddess. When the Ephesians stopped worshiping Artemis and started worshiping Jesus, the economic vitality of the idol factories was threatened. To preserve their way of life, the artisans tried to silence Paul and to run him out of town. The idol makers aligned their interests with Satan by opposing the exclusive worship of God. So, they stirred up a riot to resist the advancement of the church.

Paul also encouraged disciples in Rome to preach the gospel of Jesus Christ, provoking them to carry out Jesus' mission. He reminded them to liberate captives through the proclamation of the gospel. "How then will they call on him in whom they have not believed? And how are they to believe in him of whom they have never heard? And how are they to hear without someone preaching? And how are they to preach unless they are sent?" (Romans 10:14-15).

Paul provoked the early church to go on the offensive, taking the good news about Jesus into the world. Some people received the gospel and joined Jesus in his missionary endeavors. Others felt their way of life was threatened by God's Kingdom and revolted against him. The Kingdom of God and the principalities of the world oppose one another, each vying for our allegiance.

The stories we find in the early church are instructive for us today. Are we willing to enter into areas of spiritual darkness with the light of Jesus Christ? Are we ready to confront the principalities that oppose Jesus and the advancement of his church? When Eddie and I boarded the plane to Sudan, neither of us knew that our trip would be a catalyst for mission work. Our first trip to Sudan was an act of faith. It increased our willingness to accept risk for the sake of growing God's kingdom. We returned to our church asking people to pray for the Fur people. Eddie made plans to return.

When Eddie was finally able to reach the Fur people, he found a hunger for the gospel. After he was forced to leave, Fur believers continued to share the gospel among their own people. There is a growing discipleship movement among the Fur people today. Despite the setbacks he faced, Eddie was faithful to storm the gates of Hell, proclaiming the gospel of salvation among the Fur people.

A couple of blocks away from my house is a track where women are trafficked for sex. My friends Tricia and Lacey started a drop-in center where women can get food, a hot shower, and have a safe place to socialize. When women are ready, my friends help them to escape from their entrapment in the sex industry. Like the slave owner in Ephesus, the men who manage these women for sexual exploitation are often enraged that they've lost a source of income. My friends, and the women they help, live under threat of retaliation. Helping the women to find their identity in Christ is a long, often painful process. But the power of Christ to heal the traumas these women have experienced is real. Tricia and Lacey are storming the gates of Hell. They offer liberation through Christ to women who are trapped in spiritual oppression.

People Under Authority

Eddie, Tricia, and Lacey are the church. They are people who recognize the authority of Jesus and have chosen to surrender themselves to his leadership and mission. The church is comprised of men and women who receive Jesus as their Savior and implement his teaching.

The text leading up to Matthew 16:18 helps us to better understand the nature of the church as people under God's authority. Jesus asked his disciples, "Who do people say that the Son of Man is?" And they said, "Some say John the Baptist, others say Elijah, and others Jeremiah or one of the prophets." He said to them, "But who do you say that I am?" Simon Peter replied, "You are the Christ, the Son of the living God." And Jesus answered him, "Blessed are you, Simon Bar-Jonah! For flesh and blood has not revealed this to you, but my Father who is in heaven." (Matthew 16:13-17).

Jesus refers to himself as the "Son of Man" eighty times in the Gospels. The title comes from Daniel 7:13-14. Daniel sees "one like a son of man" who appears before the Ancient of Days. The Ancient of Days gives to the Son of Man "all power and authority over every tribe, tongue, and nation on earth." Jesus is the Son of Man, who has been given authority by God, the Ancient of Days, to rule over every people group on earth. The title "Son of Man" is more than a description of Jesus' humanity. It is a proclamation of Jesus' right to govern all God's creation.

When Peter confesses that Jesus is the Messiah, the Son of the Living God, he is making a proclamation of faith. He is making a definitive statement about the authority of Jesus. Peter's revelation about Jesus' authority is a gift from God. Apart from God's grace, we cannot see Jesus for who he is. We will not recognize his authority to govern our lives apart from God's grace.

Imagine for a moment that you and I decide to partner together as missionaries to the Fur people in Sudan. We travel to the region of Darfur and construct a small building to host our worship services. We pray, sing, and study the scriptures together. Have we established the church among the Fur people? I would say no. God establishes his church among the Fur people when they comprehend the authority of Jesus and submit to him in faith.

The church is established when God reveals the identity of his Son to people. Jesus is the Lamb of God who takes away the sins of the world (John 1:29). He is the Messiah who establishes God's kingdom on earth (Psalm 8:6). He is the Son of Man who governs all nations and will judge all people (Matthew 25:31-31; John 5:22). He is the Son of the Living God (John 20:31), the second person of the trinity, God in the flesh (John 1:14). God gave his son Jesus a mission: to subdue all God's enemies and to establish God's eternal reign on earth (1 Corinthians 15:25-28). The church cannot exist apart from Jesus' leadership (1 Corinthians 12:12–12:27).

When Eddie and his team engage people with the gospel of Jesus, they ask God to reveal Himself to the people with whom they are working. Next, the team searches for an individual or family who is open to learning stories from the Bible that reveal Jesus' authority. Those who come to faith receive repeated exposure to God's word, and they often have dreams of Jesus.

The Holy Spirit encourages people to be curious about the Bible. People explore God's word in small groups with their family members, friends, and other members of their community. After wrestling with the authority of God's word, they count the cost of persecution for leaving the Muslim faith. Some become convinced of the truth of the Bible and surrender their lives to Jesus. Often times, the entire group decides to follow the teachings of Jesus. Previous skepticism is overcome by their faith in Jesus. They believe that Jesus died so they might have life and be restored in relationship with God. A mark of their new life in Christ includes obeying Jesus' teaching to love one another.

Now, let's look at another example of church formation. Instead of traveling to Darfur, imagine we decide to attend a local congregation in the United States. We gather together with a group of people every Sunday. We sing songs and listen to sermons. During the week, we tutor children in our local elementary school. We try our best to love our neighbors well. But as a congregation, we deny that Jesus is Lord. "Jesus is the way of salvation for some people," we say, "but there are many paths to God. Everyone can find their own way to God if they seek God earnestly." Are we the church because we engage in religious practices, or do our beliefs about Jesus truly matter?

The church is not defined by its cultural norms or religious activities. The church is defined by its relationship to Jesus. In the example above, the congregation adopted religious practices and expressed its values in the life of its community. These are honorable attributes, but the congregation is not a church. The church does not exist apart from God's revelation of Jesus as Lord.

The Church Is Living and Active

After Peter recognized Jesus' authority, Jesus said, "And I tell you, you are Peter, and on this rock, I will build my church." Jesus uses a play on words when he gives his disciple, Simon, a new name. The name Peter is *Petros* in Greek. It is derived from the word *petra* meaning rock. In Aramaic, the common language of Israelites in Jesus' day, the word for rock was *cephas*. On several occasions, the Apostle Paul refers to Peter as Cephas, the rock (Gal 2:7-14; 1 Cor 1:11-13, 3:21, 9:5, 15:5).

Peter is the rock on which Jesus builds his church. Why is this important? Because Jesus builds his church with people, with flesh and blood, not with bricks and mortar. In his letter to the early church, Peter says, "You yourselves, like living stones, are being built up as a spiritual house to be a holy priesthood, to offer spiritual sacrifices acceptable to God through Jesus Christ." Not only is Peter the rock on which the church is built, but so am I and so are you. We are all living stones, built into a temple where the Holy Spirit resides (1 Corinthians 6:19). God builds his church with people.

The church is not static or passive like a building waiting for people to inhabit it. People are living and active, and we have the ability by God's grace to engage the world with the love of Jesus Christ. Think of how different this is from the way we talk about the church. When my daughter asks, "Are we going to church today?" I say, "No, we are the church. We are going to a worship service today with the rest of our church. When the worship service ends, the church will scatter to share God's love with our neighbors, our classmates and our co-workers."

Doctrines, or the teachings of the church, play a vital role in shaping our understanding of God and our identity in Christ. If people are the basic building blocks of the church, we can think of doctrines as a chisel in the hands of the Holy Spirit, chipping away at our misunderstandings about God and our human nature. Doctrines shape us into the people God desires us to be. But it is people, broken, fallible, sinful people that God uses to build his church.

Many people in my neighborhood are unwilling to attend a worship service until they become a better person. They feel like they need to get their act together before they present themselves to God. The idea of cleaning ourselves up for God is a lie Satan uses to keep us from receiving God's grace. The apostle Paul says that we are all sinful people. We are born as children of wrath, under the influence of Satan, the world, and our own sinful desires (Ephesians 2:1-3). There is nothing that we can do on our own to clean ourselves up for God. We are dependent upon God's grace (Ephesians 2:4). God takes the initiative to save us from our sins.

Jesus himself says that he is the good shepherd who came to seek and to save those who are lost (John 10:10). Jesus finds us in the world while we are still trying to fulfill our own sinful passions. Then Jesus calls us out of the world into a relationship with himself. The Greek word for church is *ekklesia.* The prefix "ek" means "out of." The root word *kaleo* means "to call." The church is comprised of people who have been called out of the world. We have been set apart from the world to honor Jesus with our lives.

Making a break with sinful patterns in our lives is not a prerequisite for our participation in the church. As we learn to submit to the power of God, we will reflect God's character more and more. Like Peter, we enter into a relationship with God through a confession of faith, not through our weak attempts to fulfill God's righteousness.

When we receive Jesus as our Lord and Savior, we receive his righteousness. Jesus restores our relationship to God. Now that our relationship is restored, we have fellowship with God. As we learn to submit to the Spirit of God, God reproduces his character in us (Gal 5:16-19). Through the power of the Holy Spirit, we are able to do good works that bring glory and honor to God (Eph 2:10; Matthew 5:16). Now we are empowered to fulfill Jesus' commands to love and forgive, to be generous and hospitable, to be humble and gracious to others. Living by an ethic of love is possible now for broken, sinful people.

The Reality of Suffering

In some ways, we've flipped the New Testament's portrayal of the church on its head. Instead of understanding the church as the people of God who storm the gates of Hell with the good news of God's Kingdom, we've built our own walled cities to protect ourselves from our enemies. We call these church buildings sanctuaries, signifying our retreat from the world into places of safety. Our concept of mission has been reduced to two-week trips where we do good works before retreating into our spiritual compounds again. We endanger God's mission by retreating from the prevailing culture instead of engaging it with the gospel of Jesus Christ.

Paul and Silas took the gospel to the marketplace in Ephesus. There were clear signs of repentance within the prevailing culture because of their ministry. But, they also experienced hostility from those who held fast to their pagan beliefs. If we faithfully engage the world with the gospel today, shouldn't we expect the same? A mixture of spiritual fruitfulness and suffering?

Will the church of the 21st century be able to shift its paradigm from seeking sanctuary from the world to storming the gates of Hell? Can we recover the church as the people of God set apart from the world, yet living by God's grace in it? Are we prepared to suffer for our faith as we follow Jesus into the world, seeking allegiance to his Kingdom?

Satan protects his strongholds. He doesn't want to release his captives to Jesus and his emissaries, the church. Missionaries from our church suffer under harsh living conditions and hostile spiritual environments. Eddie and his team have set aside creaturely comforts to live among a remote people who don't know anything about Jesus and the salvation he provides. Performing the very basic tasks of cooling their home and preparing food for their families takes tremendous effort. The threat of death is great for those who choose to hear their message and respond in faith. New believers have been imprisoned and tortured for refusing to recant their faith in Jesus.

Jesus warned his disciples about the reality of suffering for their faith. After Jesus commended Peter for his proclamation of faith, Jesus warned his disciples about the suffering that awaited them. Jesus said he would be arrested and put to death by the religious leaders in Jerusalem.

Peter responded by rebuking Jesus saying, "Far be it from you, Lord! This shall never happen to you" (Matthew 16:22). To which Jesus replies, "Get behind me, Satan! You are a hindrance to me. For you are not setting your mind on the things of God, but on the things of man. If anyone would come after me, let him deny himself and take up his cross and follow me. For whoever would save his life will lose it, but whoever loses his life for my sake will find it" (Matthew 16:23-24). If the church hopes to recover the integrity of its mission, we must recover an ethic of suffering and personal sacrifice.

Initially, Peter doesn't have the insight to see what lies beyond Jesus' suffering and death. He views Jesus' crucifixion as a defeat, a tragic end to the establishment of his kingdom on earth. Sometime later in his life, Peter comes to a proper understanding of Jesus' sacrifice. He writes, "He himself bore our sins in his body on the tree, that we might die to sin and live to righteousness. By his wounds you have been healed" (1 Peter 2:24). Peter finally recognized that Jesus' suffering was necessary for our healing.

Jesus calls us to follow in his footsteps by taking up our cross and following him (Matthew 16:24). Suffering is not an affliction to be avoided; it is the natural consequence of the church engaging the world as a part of Christ's mission. Jesus tells his disciples, "Blessed are you when people revile you and persecute you and utter all kinds of evil against you falsely on my account. Rejoice and be glad, for your reward is great in heaven" (Matthew 5:11-12).

Our suffering is a sign that we have rightly aligned ourselves with Christ against the powers and principalities of the world. Our suffering is a natural consequence of refusing to conform to the values of the world. Peter echoes the teaching of Jesus when he says that God will bless those who suffer for doing what is right (1 Peter 3:16-17). Paul also encourages new disciples by reminding them, "It is through many persecutions that we must enter the kingdom of God" (Acts 14:22). Suffering at the hands of God's enemies is a normal part of the Christian faith.

In order for the church to fulfill its mission, we must embrace a proper understanding of suffering. Otherwise, we will be tempted to quit when the going gets tough. God is sending us into spiritually dark places to share the light of Christ. When we do so, suffering will result. As we share the hope we have in Christ with those who are opposed to Christ's rule, a cultural backlash may ensue. Paul was often beaten and run out of town for his testimony about Jesus. We should expect the same.

God is sending his church into the world to liberate people from their bondage to Hell, just as Jesus did with the early church. Our mission is the same: to make disciples of all nations teaching people to obey Jesus. The church will complete its mission when people from every tribe, tongue, and nation worship the Lamb who was slain for their sins (Revelation 7:9-10), confessing that Jesus is Lord (Philippians 2:10-11), living in humble submission to the Spirit of God (Galatians 5:16), while putting God's ethic of love into practice (Colossians 3:1-17).

Until that day comes, we are to storm the gates of Hell, battering down its lies with the truth of God's word. As we do so, Hell's gates will give way to Christ's kingdom. People will be transformed by God's grace. Empowered by the Holy Spirit, a new generation of Christ-followers will begin to transform the world around them as Jesus' love finds expression through their actions. The kingdom of God will break into the world where Hell once held it captive.

Questions for Reflection

1. What does Jesus mean when he says, "The gates of Hell will not prevail against the church?"
2. In what ways do you see the powers and principalities of Hell embedded in human culture?

3. How is your church engaging the world as an agent of God's grace?

CHAPTER 2

YOU ARE CALLED

"For consider your calling, brothers: not many of you were wise according to worldly standards, not many were powerful, not many were of noble birth. But God chose what is foolish in the world to shame the wise; God chose what is weak in the world to shame the strong."
1 Corinthians 1:26-27

When Kim and I first moved to the inner city, an acquaintance of ours thanked us for the personal sacrifices we were making. She said, "I'm so glad God called you to move into Binghampton. You must have a very special calling to do what you do." Other friends made similar comments. "I could never do what you are doing. I am so thankful for God's calling on your life." I might not have been interpreting their comments correctly, but it seemed to me that people were implying, "I'm glad God called you to that ministry and not me."

I felt like people were using a lack of "calling" as an excuse for spiritual complacency and as a license to pursue their self-interests. I started questioning the idea of calling altogether. Was "calling" a Biblical concept? Was it a cultural construct used to describe why some people go into full-time Christian ministry and others do not? Did the idea of calling move people to greater faithfulness in their walk with God? Did a lack of calling excuse people from addressing difficult problems in society?

I was given an opportunity to explore these questions in greater depth when I worked as a faculty member for Resurrection Health, a Christian medical residency program. One of my responsibilities was to host visiting medical students during their primary care rotations with our clinic. The medical students would receive training in the morning with their supervising physicians. I would meet with them in the afternoon to discuss ways they could serve Christ through their vocation. We talked about how to use the practice of medicine to honor God.

Our conversations usually started with the students telling me why they decided to enter the medical field. They would say mundane things like, "I was drawn to the science of medicine" or "I wanted to help people." Then I would ask, "Why does God want you to be a doctor?" I received a lot of blank stares. Many of the students had never considered how their careers could further the purposes of God.

Most of the time we don't distinguish between the words *occupation* and *vocation*, but they have distinct meanings. An occupation is a job that "occupies" our time and supplies for our needs. A vocation carries the nuance of personal suitability to the work we do and of dedication to a higher purpose that supersedes our own desires. Christians don't have occupations; we have vocations. As Christians we don't just work; we work for God. The Bible instructs followers of Jesus to be intentional about their work. "Whatever you do, in word or deed, do everything in the name of the Lord Jesus, giving thanks to God the Father through him" (Colossians 3:17).

Over the years, I have had the opportunity to talk to hundreds of Christian medical students as they wrestle with the idea of calling. I try to help them see that medicine should not be pursued for the lifestyle it can provide but for the purpose it can fulfill in God's mission to the world. Our conversations were as helpful for me as they were for the students. They helped me to unpack the idea of a calling in my own life. Those conversations forced me to look beyond our day-to-day use of the term calling and to reexamine its Biblical roots.

Called into a Relationship with God

God calls people to abandon their pursuit of worldly passions to love God and to serve Him. Calling is not reserved for pastors, ministers, and missionaries. Every Christian is called out of the world and into a relationship with Jesus. We have been set apart from the world to serve God's purposes.

Genesis 11:4 paints a picture of the world pursuing its own self-interests. "Come, let us build ourselves a city and a tower with its top in the heavens, and let us make a name for ourselves, lest we are dispersed over the face of the whole earth." The Babylonian people built a tower as a testimony to their greatness. God was displeased with their pride. Instead of worshiping God, devoting themselves to his service, they lived to serve their own greatness.

In Genesis 12:1-2, God tells a man named Abram (later called Abraham) to leave his home in Babylon behind. "Go from your country and your kindred and your father's house to the land that I will show you. And I will make you a great nation, and I will bless you and make your name great so that you will be a blessing." God calls Abraham to leave the worldly pursuits of the Babylonians behind to pursue *God's purposes*. God invites Abraham and his descendants, the Israelites, into a special relationship with himself.

After rescuing them from their slavery in Egypt, God told the Israelites, "You yourselves have seen what I did to the Egyptians, and how I bore you on eagles' wings and brought you to myself. Now, therefore, if you will indeed obey my voice and keep my covenant, you shall be my treasured possession among all people, for all the earth is mine; and you shall be to me a kingdom of priests and a holy nation" (Exodus 19:4-6).

Calling is first and foremost about our relationship with God. God wanted to have a relationship with Abraham and the Israelites that was different from the way people related to one another in the world.

Instead of pursuing personal glory, as the Babylonians and Egyptians did, the Israelites were to be a "holy nation." To be holy means to be set apart. God set the Israelites apart from the world to serve his purposes. They were to find their glory in their service to God, by obeying his commandments. As a nation, they were called to serve God as a kingdom of priests, reflecting God's judgments and values in the world around them.

The apostle Paul built on the story of Israel's calling in 1 Corinthians 1:1-31, extending the theme of calling to his fellow Christians. Paul used the term *calling* four different times, each time building on principles that were revealed through Israel's relationship with God in the Old Testament.

Paul says God called us into fellowship with Jesus (1 Corinthians 1:9; Exodus 19:4,6). He called us to be holy (1 Corinthians 1:2; Exodus 19:6). God called us to serve Him with our spiritual gifts (1 Corinthians 1:1; Exodus 19:5). Finally, God calls ordinary people to display God's extraordinary grace in the world around them (1 Corinthians 1:27; Deuteronomy 7:7).

Paul reminded the church that they were called into a relationship with Jesus. "God is faithful, by whom you were called into fellowship with Jesus Christ, our Lord" (1 Corinthians 1:9). As we attempt to discern God's calling for our lives, we must first remember that God's will is to bring us into his family. "But to all who did receive him, who believed in his name, he gave the right to become children of God, who were born, not of blood nor of the will of the flesh nor of the will of man, but of God" (John 1:12-13). God chose us to be a part of his family. God adopted us as his children and placed us under the authority of Jesus, the master of God's house (Hebrews 3:6). Our relationship to Jesus should define the way we live.

Jesus has been given the right to rule God's creation. "For by him, all things were created, in heaven and on earth, visible and invisible, whether thrones or dominions or rulers or authorities—all things were created through him and for him" (Colossians 1:16). We were created by Jesus to serve his purposes. We should use the influence and authority that we have been given to institute Jesus' purposes in the world around us.

One day, everyone will recognize Jesus' authority and will submit to him. "For this reason also, God highly exalted Him, and bestowed on Him the name which is above every name, so that at the name of Jesus every knee will bow, of those who are in heaven and on earth and under the earth, and that every tongue will confess that Jesus Christ is Lord, to the glory of God the Father" (Philippians 2:9-11). We should recognize Jesus' authority in our lives by surrendering to his leadership.

God appointed Jesus as head of the church. "He put all things under his feet and gave him as head over all things to the church" (Ephesians 1:20). Jesus has authority over every denomination, every church congregation, and every ministry endeavor. All our decisions as a church should reflect Jesus' priorities as the leader of our congregations.

We enter into a saving relationship with Jesus through faith in him. "If you confess with your mouth Jesus as Lord, and believe in your heart that God raised Him from the dead, you will be saved" (Romans 10:9). Jesus is our Lord and Savior. He provides his followers with forgiveness from their sins and grants us eternal life. Jesus has saved us for a purpose: to be in a relationship with him for all eternity.

Just as we surrender to Jesus acknowledging him as our savior, we should also surrender our way of life to him. Every area of relationship and responsibility should be marked by Jesus' authority over our lives. His character and purposes should be reflected in the way we parent our children, interact with our co-workers, and carry out our responsibilities. Jesus is the Lord of every aspect of our lives.

Finally, Jesus is our deliverer. Satan opposes Jesus and his church, but Jesus will deliver us from the evil one. "These will wage war against the Lamb, and the Lamb will overcome them, because He is Lord of lords and King of kings, and those who are with Him are the called and chosen and faithful" (Revelation 17:14). Despite the persecution we face from the spiritual forces of evil, we persevere with Christ in overcoming the evil one. Jesus will deliver us from our enemies. We are called by God into a saving relationship with Jesus and empowered by his Spirit to overcome our adversaries.

Remember how Jesus promised that the gates of Hell will not prevail against the church? The church will prevail in its mission because we are under the authority of the Lamb of God who will overcome the evil one. Jesus ensures our ultimate victory as we storm the gates of Hell. We have been called to take up our cross and follow Jesus, dying to our own agenda to take up his agenda for our lives.

Called to Be Holy

Not only are we called into fellowship with Jesus, but God also calls us to be holy. "To the church of God in Corinth, to those sanctified in Christ Jesus and called to be his holy people" (1 Corinthians 1:2). God calls us out of the world, separating us from the pursuit of worldly power, pleasure, and prestige. Instead of seeking our own gratification, we pursue God's agenda and serve at his pleasure.

There is another "churchy" word that helps us to understand God's calling. *Sanctification* means to make something holy or to separate something from the ordinary. There were many holy objects used for worship in the tabernacle: a golden lampstand (Exodus 37:17-24), sacred anointing oil (Exodus 30:22-33) and holy incense (Exodus 30:34-38). These objects were set apart from ordinary use. They were only used to worship God. If an Israelite used the sacred incense as a personal perfume, he was ostracized from the community (Exodus 30:38). The sacred objects served a single purpose: to honor God in worship.

Sanctification is the process God uses to separate us from an "ordinary life" so that we will serve Him, reflecting God's values and accomplishing God's purposes in the world. Those whom God sanctifies are called saints in the Bible, or holy people. Their purpose in life has changed. Saints no longer pursue a personal agenda. They live for the sole purpose of serving God.

Now here is the important part that most of us miss: every Christian is made holy by God. In the Old Testament, the priesthood was set apart to serve God, attending to the sacrifices and worship in the Tabernacle. But in the New Testament, every Christian is called by God and separated from the world to serve God's purposes. "You are a chosen race, a royal priesthood, a holy nation, a people for his own possession, that you may proclaim the excellencies of him who called you out of darkness into his marvelous light" (1 Peter 2:9).

God frees us from our bondage to sin, to serve his purposes by loving one another. "You, my brothers and sisters, were called to be free. But do not use your freedom to indulge the flesh; rather, serve one another humbly in love. For the entire law is fulfilled in keeping this one command: "Love your neighbor as yourself" (Galatians 5:13-14). The Holy Spirit sets us apart from the prevailing culture, convicting us of the many ways that we seek our own well-being at the expense of others. The Holy Spirit also empowers us to deny ourselves so that we will live according to God's purposes in every aspect of our lives. God wants us to love one another with the love we have received from Him.

God reveals his purposes through the Bible so will know how to live in faithful obedience to Him. Jesus prayed for his disciples, asking God to "sanctify them in the truth," reminding them, "God's word is truth" (John 17:17). We are set apart from the world to obey the teachings of Jesus as recorded in God's word. We don't need to hear a special word from the Lord to be called by God. We simply need to obey the teachings of Jesus as recorded in the Bible.

Called to Christian Service

A third usage of the term *calling* occurs in 1 Corinthians 1:1. Paul told the Corinthian church that he was called to be an apostle. The word *apostle* means "one who is sent." Jesus sent Paul to tell the good news that through Christ, God was calling people from every nation into a special relationship with himself (Acts 9:15). Paul and the other apostles and leaders of the church were tasked with the responsibility of preparing people for Christian service. "And he [Jesus] gave the apostles, prophets, evangelists, shepherds, and teachers, to equip the saints for the work of ministry" (Ephesians 4:11-12). As an apostle, Paul was responsible for equipping the saints to serve God's purposes.

If you are like me, you probably don't feel "saintly." But remember, *saint* refers to one who has been made holy or set apart for ministry. *Ministry* simply means "service." The church has been called out of the world to serve God. It is the role of Christian leaders to equip the church to serve God through many different vocations.

As followers of Jesus Christ, we have to stop separating our spiritual lives from our work. Work is one of many places where we can express our faith and calling. We need Christian men and women to integrate God's values into the marketplace. It doesn't matter if you are a doctor, lawyer, teacher, musician, etc.; all should seek to reflect God's purposes in their work.

A sanctified doctor serves other people under God's direction, reflecting God's values. Therefore, she does her work with integrity, looking to maximize God's glory rather than maximizing her own personal gain. A sanctified doctor does not pursue medicine for the lifestyle that it will afford her, but for the mission of healing people in the name of Christ.

She uses the skills she has acquired through the study of medicine to express God's love to the world. Because she has been set apart to serve Christ alone, she gives generously of her time to the poor, helping those who would otherwise be priced-out of the healthcare industry by the market economy.

The sanctified doctor is motivated by the commands of Christ and not by money. She makes room for the poor in her medical practice. When she serves those who may not be able to repay her for her services, she is serving her savior. For the Bible says, "Whatever you did for one of the least of these brothers and sisters of mine, you did for me" (Matthew 25:40).

She asks her patients if they want to receive prayer as a part of their therapeutic plan, knowing that God is the one who heals all disease (Psalm 103:3). When confronted with the certainty of death, she lets her patients know about the eternal life that is available through Jesus Christ, for God alone is able "to redeem their life from the pit" (Psalm 103:4).

Our tendency as Westerners is to separate the spiritual from the material world. This tendency is reflected in our division of labor. Many physicians I've worked with were intimidated to address the spiritual concerns of their patients. That responsibility was relegated to chaplains who specialized in spiritual care. This division between physical and spiritual realities is created by our culture and is not reflective of a Biblical worldview. As a part of the priesthood of all believers, Christian physicians have been given authority by Jesus to enter into the world of spiritual care, praying for their patients and sharing the truth of scripture.

Healthcare is not the only workplace in need of sanctified Christians. Several years ago, I had an idea to raise money for several organizations that served our community. My plan was to open a donor-advised fund at a local foundation. The fund would collect donations and distribute them at the end of each month to ten different Christian organizations. I was going to market the giving opportunity as a nonprofit mutual fund—a way for donors to diversify their giving into multiple sectors of need: community development, housing, education, healthcare, and church growth. I would validate each organization that received the donations, ensuring that the donor was maximizing the effectiveness of their gift. My plan was to market the fund through Christian financial planners. I approached several friends in the industry to discuss the feasibility of my idea. One by one they told me that it was considered taboo to discuss giving with their clients. I was confused.

"Shouldn't charitable giving be discussed as a part of your client's financial plan?" I asked.

"Only if the client brings it up."

"What about tax write-offs? Aren't there economic incentives for giving that should be discussed, so a client can make an informed decision about their financial plan?"

"You just don't understand. Nobody in the industry does this. You can't bring up giving unless your client initiates the discussion."

"Do your clients initiate discussions about giving?"

"Rarely. They come to us because they want to increase their financial returns, not give them away."

"Do you ever give recommendations for giving?"

"On a rare occasion, I might suggest for someone to open a donor-advised fund. But we won't discuss how to distribute the money from that fund."

Not to be deterred, I turned my attention to a couple of men who managed donor-advised funds in my city. I asked if they offered classes on how to give or if they provided coaching on how to determine if a nonprofit was making a measurable social impact. Both organizations provided their fund holders with lists of charitable organizations in the city, but neither provided direct advice on charitable giving. No one in the financial sector was talking about giving.

A friend of mine who worked for years as a bond broker recently started a fund to accelerate giving to organizations in our city. He hired a small team of financial analysts to work with nonprofits to improve their social impact. He collected donations and distributed them immediately to high-impact, non-profit organizations that were focused on alleviating poverty. He coached donors on social impact and challenged high-net-worth individuals to put their money to work in the non-profit sector rather than storing up money in their donor-advised funds. He is a prophetic voice within the industry, challenging his peers to put their faith into action through charitable giving.

He is not a pastor, but he is a minister of God's grace in the financial sector. He understands how money works and helps others become better stewards of the resources that God has entrusted to them. He is challenging the financial industry to act in ways that reflect the principles of God's kingdom.

Can you see it yet? Do you see how Satan attempts to deceive us by encouraging us to separate our work from God's influence? Jesus has called us to a different way of life. Our work should reflect our relationship with Jesus. He has set us apart to serve his purposes. Jesus desires for his presence to be experienced in your exam room and his generosity to be expressed through your financial plans. Of course, it is taboo for a doctor to pray with her patient or a financial planner to encourage his client to be generous. Satan doesn't want us fulfilling God's purposes in the world. Satan has taken the world hostage and wants to keep it in bondage. We storm the gates of Hell when we submit to Jesus' authority and carry out his commands in our workplaces despite the cultural backlash we will face for doing so.

God calls ordinary people to do his work. He is not looking for superstars. God displays his power through human weakness. "For consider your calling, brothers: not many of you were wise according to worldly standards, not many were powerful, not many were of noble birth. But God chose what is foolish in the world to shame the wise; God chose what is weak in the world to shame the strong; God chose what is low and despised in the world, even things that are not, to bring to nothing things that are, so that no human being might boast in the presence of God" (1 Corinthians 1:26-29).

Jesus is the one who made us acceptable to God. He made us holy. He gave himself to buy our freedom (1 Timothy 2:6). God chooses to display his power through weak vessels (2 Corinthians 4:7-9). We can do nothing apart from God displaying his power through us. This was not just true of the Corinthians; it's true for us today, and it has been true throughout the history of Israel and throughout the history of Christianity. Don't make excuses, saying, "I'm not called." If you are a Christian, you are called to serve God. And if you are a weak, frail Christian, who doubts your own ability to do anything of significance for God, then you are in really good company.

Moses was an ex-con with a stuttering problem. God called Moses to confront Pharaoh, the most powerful man on the planet at the time. He chose what was weak to shame the strong. Through Moses, God displayed his power by sending ten plagues on Egypt because Pharaoh refused to release God's people from captivity.

Moses didn't want to go when he received the call. Egypt was a dangerous place. If he returned to Egypt, he would be in danger of being enslaved with the rest of his kinsfolk. He was safe in Midian, on the outskirts of the Egyptian empire. He had a family with great in-laws. His life was comfortable.

So, Moses gave excuses for not going to Egypt. He had a stuttering problem. No one would believe that God had sent him to speak on God's behalf. God empowered Moses by addressing his concerns. He told Moses that his brother Aaron could speak on his behalf. God gave Moses the power to do miracles to prove that God had sent him, yet Moses still refused to go. God was angered by Moses' disobedience, but finally, Moses relented. Moses submitted to God and obeyed his commands.

As we grow in our faith, we come to understand that Christianity involves more than confessing our sins and being forgiven. We are to live by God's purposes, which involves dying to ourselves and living for Christ, by the power of his Spirit. Obedience is uncomfortable. At times, it is frightening. It is natural for us to wrestle with God as we discern his calling in our lives. Ultimately, we must come to a place of submission and surrender to his will. Despite wrestling with God, Moses was faithful and obedient to God's commands.

Another important aspect of Moses' calling was his recognition of God's holiness. God called Moses from a burning bush that was not consumed and said, "Take off your shoes, Moses, for you are standing on holy ground." Moses received a revelation of the holiness of God.

This is a common theme throughout the call narratives in the Bible. God displays his power and authority. The individual recognizes his sin and God's holiness. Most of the time, there is a brief period of wrestling with God before coming to a place of submission and obedience. God then goes on to display his power through the weakness of the individual.

One of the strongest examples of this pattern can be seen in the life of Gideon. Like Moses, Gideon was living in a time of political oppression. This time, Midian was waging war on Israel, burning their crops and slaughtering their livestock. While Gideon was working, an angel of the Lord called out to him, "Mighty warrior!"

Gideon replied, "Who me? I am the weakest man in my clan, and my clan is the weakest in my tribe, and my tribe is the weakest in Israel, and Israel is the smallest and weakest nation on Earth" (Judges 6:15). It is as if Gideon was saying, "You must be mistaken, God. I don't know who this mighty warrior is that you are talking about. I am the weakest man on Earth."

Again God chose to display his power through human weakness. God gave Gideon the task of attacking the Midianite army with only 200 men, displaying his power through the weakness of Gideon's army. God prepared Gideon for this ministry by first giving Gideon a smaller task to complete. This is instructive for us. We normally don't jump into the fullness of our calling. God gives us ministry tasks to prepare us for the work we will do. God gave Gideon a task to teach him how to walk by faith and not by fear.

God told Gideon to tear down the altar that his father built for Baal, one of the gods of Canaan. Gideon was reluctant to do so, fearful that the community would retaliate for tearing down one of their altars. So, he took ten men with him in the middle of night to tear down the altar. The next morning, Gideon's worst fears were realized. The townsfolk came after Gideon for tearing down their altar. God saved Gideon by granting his father repentance for his sinful worship practices. Gideon's father protected him by turning away the wrath of the town. He refused to allow its enraged citizens to touch his son.

Like Moses, despite his initial reluctance, Gideon was faithful and obedient to God's command. In fact, he was courageous, even though Gideon appeared cowardly by sneaking out under the cover of night to complete his task. He was obedient despite his fear. Obedience in the face of fear is the very definition of courage. Gideon learned to confront his fear with faith. In doing so, Gideon was being prepared to take on an even greater task, with more significant outcomes.

Many of us are in the same place as Gideon right now. We are in a stage of preparation. We may not be serving in the capacity we think we should or will one day. We should take every opportunity to be faithful to God now, regardless of our circumstances or the size of the task at hand. God gives us more responsibility as we are faithful with the small tasks he entrusts to us.

I have a good friend who started two different Christian medical clinics. The first grew to serve over 60,000 patients a year. When he was in medical school, his Sunday school teacher challenged him to teach a Bible study in a local housing project. At first, he didn't want to go. He wrestled with the idea. He was busy with his studies, and initially he was fearful of the community. Teaching a Bible Study didn't match his desire to serve people through medicine. Ultimately, he came to a point of surrender and taught the Bible study despite his initial misgivings. Each week that he returned to the apartment complex, his fears subsided a little more. Through this experience, he learned to overcome fear with faith. God built upon a foundation of faithfulness, progressively giving him more responsibilities and more opportunities to serve God's purposes.

Overcoming fear with faith is an essential building block for fruitful ministry. We have seen this principle played out many times throughout the course of our ministry. A young student who was studying to become a physician's assistant moved into a guest house we owned to host medical students in the inner city. The community had a bad reputation for violence. One night, close to Halloween, she called me in a panic. One of her neighbors, who some thought was a drug dealer, built a haunted maze out of old wooden pallets in the empty lot next to her house. It was no ordinary maze. It was huge. Slightly wider than a single-story house, it engulfed the entire lot. He put a coffin in it. As children from the neighborhood walked through the maze, someone would jump out of the coffin with a chainsaw.

She asked me, "What should I do? Should I call the police?" I told her to embrace it as a ministry opportunity. "Bake cookies for the kids and pass them out while they wait to go through the maze." And that's exactly what she did. She baked cookies and bought face paint and played with the kids while they waited for their turn in the maze. At one point, the generator that powered an inflatable castle at the entrance to the maze went out. My friend didn't miss a beat. She plugged the extension cord into her house and won the affection of her neighbor who was managing the maze. They became great friends after that. By loving and serving her neighbor, she overcame her fear and established a foundation for future ministry opportunities.

God is constantly presenting us with small opportunities for faithful service. They may not feel like they are a part of a greater calling at the time, but they are vital to fruitful ministry. Jesus said, "The one who is faithful in very little is also faithful in much" (Luke 16:10). We should take every opportunity to prepare ourselves for greater fruitfulness.

Responding to God's Call

Isaiah's calling followed the same pattern we've established with other faithful servants in the Bible. Like Moses and Gideon before him, Isaiah's calling begins with a revelation concerning the holiness of God. God is enthroned in his temple, surrounded by angelic beings that cry out, "Holy, holy, holy is the Lord of hosts; the whole earth is full of his glory!" (Isaiah 6:3). Upon seeing the holiness of God, Isaiah is immediately convicted of his own sin and weakness. "Woe is me! For I am lost; for I am a man of unclean lips, and I dwell in the midst of a people of unclean lips; for my eyes have seen the King, the Lord of hosts!" (Isaiah 6:5).

In the Bible, you never want to be on the wrong side of a "woe." It is a proclamation of judgment and usually means you are about to get zapped. Instead of getting zapped, God sent an angel with a burning coal from the altar to cleanse Isaiah's lips. Again we see the pattern of being called to holiness. God is equipping his saint for ministry by forgiving his sin and setting him apart for service. Then God asks, "Whom shall I send, and who will go for us?" And Isaiah responds, "Here I am! Send me" (Isaiah 6:8).

I love these stories because I can relate to them. God chooses sinful, weak people to serve him. Other than Jesus, there are no true heroes in the Bible. Everyone has shortcomings, yet God chooses to display his power through their weaknesses.

Isaiah's story holds a special place for me. Unlike Gideon and Moses, Isaiah does not respond to a job description. At this point in the story, God hasn't told Isaiah what he is supposed to do. Isaiah responds to the holiness of God. It is as if Isaiah is saying, "Whatever the job is, Lord, now that I have seen your holiness, your power, and your goodness, and now that I understand your authority, I'll do whatever you ask of me." This is the stance we should strive for as we humble ourselves before the Lord our God.

Isaiah gets the crummiest job description in the Bible. God tells him to preach a message to his kinsman that will ensure they experience the full measure of God's wrath (Isaiah 6:9-13). Isaiah's calling is not driven by his passions or desires. His actions are not rooted in his gifts or abilities. Isaiah is a weak vessel, submitted to God, serving at God's pleasure. Such submission takes humility. Humility is born out of a revelation of God's holiness, our sinfulness, and the grace we receive from our King.

Isaiah didn't experience a lot of fruit from his ministry during his lifetime. But thousands of years later, we still treasure his words. Every Christmas, we celebrate Isaiah's prophecies of the Messiah who reigns over God's kingdom. "For unto us a child is born, to us, a son is given, and the government shall be upon his shoulders, and his name shall be called Wonderful Counselor, Mighty God, Everlasting Father, Prince of Peace. Of the increase of his government and of peace, there will be no end" (Isaiah 9:6-7).

We also treasure Isaiah's prophecy of the suffering servant. "He was pierced for our transgressions; he was crushed for our iniquities; upon him was the chastisement that brought us peace, and with his wounds we are healed" (Isaiah 53:5). People all over the world have listened to Isaiah's prophecies and repented of their sins because God worked through a weak but willing vessel. God may be calling you to a seemingly fruitless ministry. You may never experience the fullness of seeing others come to faith in Christ, or to experience spiritual transformation in your home or workplace, but you are still called to be faithful. You never know how the seeds of your faithfulness will grow in the generations to come.

In a similar way, the first missionaries to China saw very little fruit from their labor, but they faithfully paved the way for preaching the gospel in Asia. In the last fifty years, China has experienced one of the largest church-planting movements in history. Those early missionaries didn't see people coming to Christ in droves. They toiled and suffered and gave their life for Christ because God called them to surrender to his Lordship. They trusted that God's plan was bigger than what they could see for themselves. Those early missionaries were weak but faithful servants of God. They surrendered their lives to Jesus, and now, hundreds of years later, we are seeing the fruit of their labor. The same will be true for you and me as we plant seeds of faith through obedience to Christ.

So, no more excuses. You are called by God. He has adopted you into his family. Jesus is your Lord. God has set you apart from the world and made you holy. He has called you to serve him in all that you do.

I challenge you to think of a couple of ways you can integrate God's purposes into your workplace. Don't be intimidated by cultural taboos. That's just Satan's way of keeping the world in bondage. Be faithful to express God's calling in all that you do. The gates of Hell won't prevail. You are on God's winning team.

Questions for Reflection

1. Is anything preventing you from surrendering your life to Jesus? If so, what is it?
2. What does it mean for you personally to be called out of the world and into God's service?
3. How can you use your work to further God's kingdom?

CHAPTER 3

PRAY FOR GOD'S KINGDOM

"Pray then like this: Our Father in heaven, hallowed be your name. Your kingdom come, your will be done, on earth as it is in heaven."
Matthew 6:9-10

It's hard not to notice when twenty Africans are walking down your street garbed in traditional clothing. We were singing songs during one of our Sunday morning house-church gatherings when one of my children called my attention to the scene developing outside. "Daddy, look!" Our neighbors walked onto the front porch and rang the bell. We opened the door, and several African families filed into the living room. None of them spoke a word of English. We rearranged the furniture and brought in more chairs from a room in the back of the house. They smiled and sat politely. After several unsuccessful attempts to make introductions, we continued with the worship service.

We sang, prayed, shared scripture together and prayed some more. After the service was over, our new African friends smiled again. They were very joyful people! We nodded to them politely as they filed out of the house. The rest of us looked at each other dumbfounded. Who were these people and where had they come from?

The next Sunday, our new neighbors joined us again for worship. This time, we made a more intentional effort to involve them in the service. We tried singing a couple of traditional worship songs. We sang a verse in English, stopped, nodded, and waited. They caught on, singing a verse of the song in their own language. We did the same thing when it came time to pray, inviting others to join us by smiling, nodding, and waiting. It worked. Several men and women joined us in prayer. I had no idea what they were saying, but they were saying it with power and conviction. Our hearts were warmed. At the end of the service, they filed out of the house and walked down the street, disappearing around the corner. Again, we were baffled.

Finally, in the third week of the "African visitation," one of the women in our church tried speaking in French. One of the African women screamed with delight, covering her mouth with her hands. She began speaking in French too. Soon, the two were chatting away. Everybody pelted the two women with questions: What were their names? Where were they from? How in the world did they end up at our little house church?

The story finally emerged. One of the doctors in our church and his wife had befriended a couple in our neighborhood from the Congo. Jocelyn was a Christian, and her husband Abdi was Muslim. Abdi volunteered with the local refugee resettlement office. He translated for refugee families when they went to the doctor's office for their initial health screenings. He told the families how the doctor and his wife had shown his family kindness and hospitality. He told each family he met, "You should go to church with the doctor and his wife. They will be kind to you. They will help you."

As we continued to put the pieces together, we realized that several other house churches in our network were having similar experiences. The churches were growing with refugees who had been referred by Abdi. God was using a Muslim man to grow our church! Over the course of the next several months, we scrambled to help our new friends find jobs, secure housing, and enroll their children in school. We found a couple of international college students at our local university who agreed to serve as translators in our house churches. We were beginning to grow together as an international community. After a period of prayerful reflection, I began to understand what had happened. Abdi was an answer to prayer.

Prayer Opens Our Hearts to God's Will

In the last chapter, we explored the importance of calling, recognizing that God uses weak but willing vessels to carry out his purposes in the world. In a similar fashion, the first missionary endeavors of the early church began with Jesus calling his disciples to himself (Luke 9:1). Those who heeded his call received power and authority to heal the sick and to drive out demons. The early disciples were vessels of God's grace, delivering people from the power of the evil one. Jesus' disciples stormed the gates of Hell, using the authority they had been given to free people from demonic oppression.

Jesus invites us to join his mission by praying for his kingdom (Matthew 6:10; Luke 11:2). When we pray, "Your kingdom come, your will be done, on earth as it is in heaven," we acknowledge Jesus' authority over our lives and surrender to his leadership. We repent from our sinful desire to determine our own future and to embrace God's plan for our lives. Our prayers invite God to fulfill his mission through us. The church will prevail against the gates of Hell as we carry out Jesus' command to pray for his kingdom.

Jesus instructed his first missionaries to pray for more Christian workers saying, "The harvest is plentiful, but the laborers are few. Therefore pray earnestly to the Lord of the harvest to send out laborers into his harvest" (Luke 10:2). Jesus' instruction to his disciples contained a promise, a problem, and a solution.

Jesus promised that the harvest would be plentiful. The disciples' mission would be successful. There were many people in need of deliverance from Satanic oppression. Many people needed healing. Many people needed forgiveness from their sins. Many people needed God's grace. Jesus promised to meet those needs through the faithful obedience of his church. As the church used the authority it had been given in Christ, people in the world would experience God's grace and turn to Jesus for healing.

God has prepared the hearts of many people to receive his grace and to come into his kingdom. The problem, as Jesus presents it, is that there are not enough workers to take the message of the gospel to the masses. There are not enough followers of Jesus who have heeded his call to abandon the world to pursue God's purposes.

Jesus' solution to the shortage of Christian workers is prayer. He commands his disciples to pray for laborers who will use the authority Jesus has given them to free people from their spiritual bondage. The church is to pray for more missionaries, so God's mission will advance.

Pray for Laborers from the Harvest

It is interesting to note the timing of Jesus' command to pray for laborers. Jesus has already sent his twelve disciples on their first missionary journey (Luke 9:1). Now, he gathers seventy-two of his followers to proclaim the Gospel of the Kingdom once again (Luke 10:1). As this second group of disciples prepares for their journey, Jesus instructs them to pray for more laborers to join the mission (Luke 10:2). As we engage the world in mission, we are to pray for God to raise up even more missionaries to do his work. Jesus is building a missionary movement that grows through prayer.

Missionaries from our church pray for more people to join their work on the mission field. They ask God to raise up new leaders from the villages where they are working to lead the work of evangelism and discipleship. They pray specifically for men and women with whom they have shared the gospel. They ask God to fashion new believers into missionaries, encouraging them to share their newfound faith with their friends and family members. The most effective evangelists and disciple-makers are usually those who share a cultural identity with their peers. They have less of a cultural barrier to overcome. As we pray for laborers, we should ask God to raise up Christian workers from the harvest for the harvest.

Adoniram Judson, the first protestant missionary from the United States to Burma, persevered through great hardship with only a handful of disciples to show for his effort at the end of his life. Yet one of the young Burmese men he had trained led a discipleship movement among the Kiran people after Judson's death. A hundred and seventy years later, the Kiran church is still bearing fruit in Burma and beyond. Christian workers "from the harvest" who share a cultural heritage with their peers are effective evangelists for Jesus and his kingdom.

The missionaries we support have asked us to join them in praying earnestly for more laborers. To pray earnestly means to pray with seriousness, conviction, and expectation. Members of our church gather in each other's homes, praying for several hours at a time, asking God to raise up new leaders for each of the missionaries we support. Just as Jesus expects his disciples to obey his command to pray, we expect God to answer our prayers by raising up new leaders to fulfill his mission to the nations.

Pray for Courage to Obey God's Call

As we follow Jesus' instruction to pray for more laborers to serve as missionaries, we need to be prepared to go ourselves. Praying for God's will to be done on earth as it is in heaven is an invitation to join God in his mission to the world. By obeying

Jesus' directive to pray for laborers, we align our hearts and intentions with God's own. We begin to see the world through Jesus' eyes. We see opportunities for service that we were once blinded to. Praying for laborers will open us to being sent ourselves. As the great protestant missionary William Carey said, "If you want the Kingdom speeded, go out and speed it yourselves. Only obedience rationalizes prayer. Only missions can redeem your intercessions from insincerity."

Our prayers for more laborers should be informed by God's word. We should not be under the delusion that missionary service is glamorous. It is dangerous work. As Jesus prepared the disciples for their missionary service, he warned them, "I am sending you out as lambs among wolves" (Luke 10:3).

If the church is going to be faithful to its mission, we must embrace the idea that mission work is dangerous. Love, peace, kindness, and gentleness are qualities that develop as people surrender their lives to the Holy Spirit (Galatians 5:20). Cultures that have not come under the influence of God's love are often hotbeds of hostility. Mission history is filled with stories of people entering violent and inhospitable territory for the sake of sharing God's redemptive love with its hostile inhabitants. Our prayers need to reflect the reality that God's mission is dangerous. We need to pray for courage and perseverance as we engage in God's mission.

Our small church has been privileged to prepare and send thirty-five adults overseas for service as career missionaries. For these missionaries and their families, the idea of being a lamb sent out to live among wolves is very real. Young missionaries are often idealists and naive, at times underestimating the threats inherent in their mission. They are not military special ops who have been field-tested and trained for battle. They are much more like sheep. Yet the threats they face are as real as any military opponent.

Many of our missionaries' extended family members grieve over the difficulty that a long-distance relationship with their children and grandchildren will bring. Many parents have justifiable fears of the dangers their adult children will face. Often times the commitments of the young missionary families are not aligned with those of their parents, and a period of hostility ensues. These are normal responses to the very real threats that await missionaries on the frontier. Grace is needed on both sides to work through the implications of Jesus' commandment to make disciples of all nations, as he sends his sheep into dangerous territory. We pray that God will align the hearts of parents and their adult children as we engage in God's mission together.

On several occasions, older parents who opposed their grown child's plan for missionary service became their child's staunchest supporters. Their hearts changed as they prayed for their children. Others remained resolute in their opposition, determined that their children had abandoned the safety and security that they had worked so hard to provide.

Jesus' words are important for us to consider as we prepare for his mission, "I am sending you out as lambs among wolves" (Luke 10:3). Jesus knows that he is sending us into difficult circumstances where our lives will be at risk. Knowing the risk beforehand can help us persevere in prayer through the hardships we will face as we engage in God's mission to the world.

Pray for Provision and Hospitality

So far, we've discussed praying to align our will with God's will, preparing our hearts to receive Jesus calling. We pray for more laborers so Jesus' mission will be completed by his church. We pray for courage to obey Jesus' call to serve as missionaries ourselves, overcoming the fear of danger that awaits us. Finally, we pray for God's provision, trusting that God will meet our needs as we carry out his mission to the world.

Jesus tells his disciples not to take provisions for their missionary journey. "Carry no money bag, no knapsack, no sandals, and greet no one on the road. Whatever house you enter, first say, 'Peace be to this house!' And if a son of peace is there, your peace will rest upon him. But if not, it will return to you. And remain in the same house, eating and drinking what they provide, for the laborer deserves his wages" (Luke 10:4-7).

Instead of taking money for their own financial needs, the disciples are instructed to receive the hospitality of strangers. Jesus tells his disciples that when they enter a home, they should offer a blessing of peace. If they are received into the home, they should accept the hospitality that is extended to them. Jesus calls the hospitable stranger a "son of peace." This is where the missionary concept of a person of peace originates. A person of peace facilitates God's mission by offering hospitality and provision to God's laborer. A person of peace most often shares the cultural identity of the host community and helps the missionary to fulfill his mission.

Abdi was a person of peace. Although he did not share our Christian beliefs, he was moved by our church's love for refugee families. As a refugee himself, Abdi recognized the needs of the refugee community. He experienced God's blessing through members of our church who were kind to his family. He was grateful for the hospitality that our church offered him and was eager to help us carry out our ministry of loving other refugee families. He received the peace we extended to him, and he wanted other people to experience God's blessing.

God's promise to provide for the missionary from the host community reorients our normal expectations. Relying on the host community communicates that we all have something of value to give to God's kingdom. *Reciprocity* is needed to build authentic relationships across cultural barriers. Reciprocity is defined as "the practice of exchanging things with others for mutual benefit." The disciples gave their testimony about Jesus and his Kingdom and healed the sick. The host community provided housing, food, and opportunities for relationships to develop that furthered God's mission. When both parties gave and received from one another, mutually beneficial relationships developed.

When my wife and I first moved into our urban neighborhood, we didn't have much money. We incurred a lot of debt through college and graduate school. When we moved into our first house, we didn't own a lawnmower, and we didn't have the money to pay for a regular lawn service. So, I borrowed a lawnmower from my neighbor, Mr. Thomas.

Mr. Thomas was more than willing to let me use his mower. He simply asked for me to lock it up after each use so it wouldn't get stolen. Every week, I would knock on his door to let him know I was borrowing his mower. We would talk for ten to fifteen minutes about our families and exchange news about the neighborhood. Sometimes, he would invite me in for coffee as well. I always felt bad about borrowing Mr. Thomas' lawnmower, but those feelings were 100% driven by my own pride. Mr. Thomas was always incredibly gracious to me.

One Sunday afternoon, my wife and I were eating lunch at my parents' house when their phone rang. It was Mr. Thomas. Knowing that we weren't at home, Mr. Thomas had flipped through the phone book, calling over 50 families with the last name Cook before finding my father. Water was running out from behind our house and he was desperately trying to let us know. When I got home, I discovered that our dog had figured out how to turn on the outdoor faucet with his mouth. A potential catastrophe was averted. Mr. Thomas was attentive to our needs. We were blessed to have him as our neighbor.

The next summer, I bought my own lawnmower. Mr. Thomas and I didn't have our weekly porch chats after that. He was still a great neighbor, but our relationship was never the same. At the time, I didn't realize the importance of being vulnerable with our neighbors. I didn't give them an opportunity to help us as we shared Christ's love with them. Receiving from our neighbors allowed us to stand on equal footing.

Our relationships in our neighborhood have always been more authentic when we have been vulnerable with our neighbors, allowing them to express their love for us by meeting our needs. Jesus wants us to approach mission work with the same humility and vulnerability, allowing others to meet our needs as we seek to meet the needs of others through the proclamation of the gospel. By praying for God to meet our needs through our neighbors, we prepare our hearts for humility and open our eyes to opportunities that we would normally not see.

Putting Prayer into Practice

Several years ago, our church conducted a training seminar to prepare people for missions using principles found in Luke 10. After the seminar was over, half of the group committed to putting those principles into practice over the following three months. We broke up into groups of two, sending pairs of people into the city to pray, looking for ways to bless the community and to share the good news of Jesus.

Two young engineers methodically followed the principles of prayer in Luke 10. They prayed for God to provide laborers from the harvest. They asked God to direct them to people of peace who would help them accomplish their mission. They prayed together as they walked around an apartment complex where many refugee families lived. Two girls wearing head coverings approached them and asked them what they were doing. The young engineers said, "We are with a church that wants to help refugee families. Can you introduce us to people in your community?

"Yes, of course," the women said. "We know the refugee families in this apartment complex. We will introduce you to them right now."

God answered the prayers of two engineers. The two refugee women were people of peace. They extended hospitality to the two men from our church, inviting them into the homes of several refugee families. The refugee women used their network of relationships to make connections for the young engineers who were new to their community. They provided for their needs.

Over the course of the next several hours, the two young men met with most of the families in the apartment complex, receiving cups of tea as they entered each apartment. After a couple of preliminary meetings, they finally met with the "headman" who spoke on behalf of the other families. He gave them permission to gather the families together to ask them about their needs.

The next week, the refugees met again with the two men from our church. The refugees wanted to learn English. The two men recruited a dozen volunteers, training them to teach English while sharing stories from the Bible. Over time, the refugee families grew in their understanding of the English language and American culture. The gospel was shared by the volunteers on many occasions, and Bibles were distributed in the native language of the people.

Half the families who volunteered to teach English went on to serve as long-term missionaries among unreached people groups in the years that followed. They continued to use the principles they learned in Luke 10: praying for people of peace while trusting God to provide through the hospitality of their host community. My prayer for the church today is that we would continue to obey Jesus' command to go and make disciples of all nations with the faith and dedication of those two young engineers.

The early church experienced the power of prayer as they carried out Jesus' mission to preach the gospel and to heal the sick (Luke 10:19). God's mission in the world still advances as missionaries faithfully obey Jesus' command to go and make disciples of all nations. But the great commission is not a specialized calling for individuals; it is a command given by Jesus to his church. It is our duty to obey, and our obedience starts with praying for laborers.

The apostle Paul said, "Faith comes from hearing the message, and the message is heard through the word about Christ" (Romans 10:17). God's kingdom grows through the preaching and proclamation of the gospel. We must hear it before we can believe it. And to hear it, we need people who will proclaim it.

I fear that our churches have become so preoccupied with our own problems and agendas that we have lost sight of Jesus' mission for his church. We lack the missionaries we need to complete Jesus' command to make disciples of all nations because we have stopped praying for more laborers.

People will not respond in faith to become missionaries until they hear the words of Matthew 28 and Luke 10 preached consistently. As we hear God's word, we must humble ourselves, lay down our personal agendas and submit our lives to God's direction. We must pray for God's will to be done, and not our own.

Fulfilling Jesus' mission starts by heeding his command to pray for more laborers. Would you be willing to organize a small group of people in your church to pray regularly for the nations, asking God to raise up more laborers to complete the Great Commission?

Questions for Reflection

1. What is your church's strategy for completing the Great Commission?
2. How can Luke 10 be used to inform your strategy for prayer?
3. JoshuaProject.net lists ethnic groups who still don't know Jesus. Will you consider praying for one of these groups regularly with your church or small group?

CHAPTER 4

HOW TO OBEY GOD

"I will put my Spirit within you, and cause you to walk in my statutes and be careful to obey my rules."
Ezekiel 36:27

It was a typical evening in the South. I was sitting on my porch, drinking a glass of sweet tea, watching the evening sky erupt in colors of pink, blue and orange as the sun set in front of me. A gentle breeze broke the sweltering humidity that settles in Memphis every spring and lingers through to Thanksgiving Day. But the peacefulness of my surroundings was disrupted by a recurring thought: *who are these people?*

We lived at the end of a cul de sac, and I rarely saw strangers walking through our neighborhood, but that night, I was seeing a lot of people I didn't know on our street. They were knocking on the door of the lime green house three doors down from us. One after another they would enter the house and promptly leave a few minutes later, racing out of the neighborhood as quickly as they came.

Instinctively, I knew what was happening, but I didn't want to believe it. I called my friend Marlon, affectionately known as Big Dog, to get the low down.

"What am I watching, Marlon?" I asked.

"You've got a drug house on your street."

And that was the end of our conversation. I poured out the rest of my tea onto our overgrown azaleas and walked back inside for the night.

The next morning, the elders of our church met for our regular time of prayer. Eric was a close friend, a fellow elder, and the executive director of Service Over Self, a home repair ministry that served our community. Before we prayed together, he briefly shared some of the things he had been learning while studying the book of Ezekiel. I don't remember the specifics, but "Ezekiel" was planted in my head. After our formal time of prayer together, I found a private room and continued to pray for my neighborhood.

As I prayed, I was plagued by thoughts of the drug house on our street. My soul was disquieted. I was having trouble focusing my prayers, so I paused, opened my Bible to Ezekiel, and was startled by what I read. "When I say to a wicked person, 'You will surely die,' and you do not warn them or speak out to dissuade them from their evil ways in order to save their life, that wicked person will die for their sin, and I will hold you accountable for their blood" (Ezekiel 3:18).

Immediately, I felt conviction from the Holy Spirit. "You are not going to hold me accountable for my neighbor's sin, are you, God?" The emotions of the night before were messing with my mind. I closed the Bible. My time of prayer was over. I didn't want to hear anything else.

Later that morning, I visited my friend Tim. Tim was an electrician in our church who suffered from severe back pain. I met with Tim at his house regularly to pray and discuss the Bible together. I told Tim about the drug house, the scripture I had read, and my time of prayer. "Do you think that God wants me to confront my neighbor about selling drugs?"

"Yes, I do. But don't worry. I'll go with you. We can do it together."

"No thanks, Tim. I don't want to get you involved in this." It was getting real now. Fear was growing in my heart. God was prompting me to confront a drug dealer face to face.

I left Tim's house and drove back to my office at SOS. Again, I met with my friend Eric, who was sitting in his office when I arrived. Eric, like me, was a seminary graduate. I thought to myself, *Surely I am taking this Ezekiel passage out of context.* God gave Ezekiel a specific calling for a specific time and place. This passage didn't apply to me. I asked Eric for his thoughts on the matter, hoping he would let me off the hook.

"Nathan, I think God is speaking to you through this passage of scripture. If you want, I'll go with you to speak to your neighbor."

"Not interested."

"Well, can I at least pray for you?"

Again, I consented. I felt the rush of the Holy Spirit in my heart. If I didn't go now, I never would, so I headed for the door.

I started feeling flush like I was going to faint. Nothing in me wanted to talk to Mario, my drug-dealing neighbor, but I couldn't overcome the feeling that I had to do so now.

I drove from SOS back to my neighborhood. I slowed down in front of Mario's house preparing to stop. Then I sped up again and pulled into my driveway. I ran into my house. Kim was at work. I was all alone. I dropped to my knees in front of our couch and cried out to God.

"Oh God, please don't make me do this!"

I got up again and walked to the door. On my way out, I saw a tract that our church had made about Adam and Eve's fall from grace. I stuffed it in my pocket and walked three doors down to Mario's house. I knocked on the door and Tamisha answered. Tamisha was Mario's fiancée. "Hey, Nathan. What can I do for you?"

I completely froze. "Do you have any prayer requests?" I blurted out. I didn't know what else to say. Tamisha responded with a list of requests, but my mind was racing, and my limbs were numb. I had no idea what she was saying. I stopped her mid-sentence.

"Tamisha, that's not really why I came by today. I've seen a lot of people coming and going from your house lately, and I think you and Mario are selling drugs. I'm here to ask you to stop. You are putting yourself and the community in harm's way."

"We haven't been selling drugs, but we did let a friend of ours sell drugs out of our house. Last night we told him he couldn't do that anymore. We made him leave."

My heart was beating out of my chest. I let out a sigh of relief. I thanked Tamisha, and then turned to go home. When I turned around, Mario was walking up the driveway.

What is Mario going to think? I thought to myself. Here I am talking to his fiancée while he's gone. I felt compelled to explain myself to him.

I told Mario that I had come by to ask him to stop selling drugs. Without even looking at Tamisha, he repeated her response almost word for word. "We are not selling drugs, but our friend was. We told him to stop." Now I felt relieved. Mario had corroborated Tamisha's story. I thanked Mario and started to walk home.

"Don't you want to come in for a minute?" Mario asked.

"Sure Mario, I can come in. Actually there is something else I'd like to share with you and Tamisha if you have a few minutes."

I took out the Bible tract from my pocket, and after sharing a few pleasantries, we dove into the story of Adam and Eve. After sharing the story, I asked a few questions.

"Mario, have you ever sinned against God as Adam and Eve did?"

"No, I can't say that I have."

Standing to her feet, Tamisha began shouting at him, "You liar! We are living in sin right now! Your wife is living in East Saint Louis!"

Mario is one of the calmest, coolest guys I've ever met. Nothing seemed to rattle him. After Tamisha's outburst, he calmly reflected, "Well, I guess I have sinned."

Mario, Tamisha, and I wrapped up our conversation and prayed together. Mario thanked me for coming and invited me to come back and share more Bible stories with them in the future. I walked home on a cloud. My fear and anxiety were replaced with peace. I felt the thick presence of the Holy Spirit resting in my soul. When I got home, I prayed and gave thanks to God.

As I prayed, I realized something significant. God didn't need me to confront Mario and Tamisha after all. They had already asked their acquaintance to stop selling drugs the very night I had observed the activity in their home. The intervention that God had orchestrated wasn't for Mario and Tamisha; it was for me. God was teaching me a lesson in obedience.

I didn't want to confront Mario and Tamisha. I was filled with fear for my personal safety. I tried to rationalize my disobedience as prudence. I thought it was not wise to confront a drug dealer, because you may get shot. God's word was more trustworthy than my reasoning, and when put into practice, it liberated me from my fear and filled me with joy. I've recounted this story many times, often with tears in my eyes. Every time I tell it, I remember the deep and abiding joy I experienced on the short walk home from Mario's house. By exercising faith in God's word, and by submitting to the Holy Spirit, I experienced the joy of obedience (Gal 5:16, 22).

Crucify the Flesh

Our sinful nature resists obeying God, so the Bible instructs us to crucify the desires of our flesh. We need the Spirit of God to help us overcome our weaknesses. When we submit to the Holy Spirit, we are able to accomplish God's purposes in the world, and the outcome of our obedience is joy.

In chapter one, we looked at how Satan usurped God's kingdom, taking people hostage and attempting to keep the church at bay. Jesus instructed Peter and the early disciples to take up their crosses and to follow him, inviting them to leave their worldly pursuits behind to join him in his mission to liberate people from the power of Satan and their bondage to sin.

Peter initially failed to recognize that the power of God's kingdom could be found through crucifixion. Jesus' crucifixion paid the indebtedness of all sinners. "He was pierced for our transgressions; he was crushed for our iniquities; upon him was the chastisement that brought us peace, and with his wounds, we are healed" (Isaiah 53:5).

Jesus invited Peter to participate in the power of God's kingdom by practicing self-denial. Jesus said, "If anyone would come after me, let him deny himself and take up his cross and follow me" (Matthew 16:24). By taking up his cross, Peter put to death his own sinful desires. He aligned himself with God's will. He fought against the sinful desires of his flesh and surrendered his life to Jesus.

In a similar manner, Paul reminded the church in Galatia that "those who belong to Christ Jesus have crucified the flesh with its passions and desires" (Galatians 5:24). When we are in Christ, our flesh is put to death. It no longer has power over us. We are no longer enslaved to its desires. Rather, our flesh has been subjected to the power of Christ in us. We have a new power at work within us that is more powerful than our sinful desires. "We know that our old self was crucified with him in order that the body of sin might be brought to nothing so that we would no longer be enslaved to sin" (Romans 6:6).

Jesus defeated the power of sin in us. Now we are free to follow Jesus, to embrace his calling, and to obey his commands. We are no longer held captive by the power of sin. As the apostle Paul says, "Let not sin therefore reign in your mortal body, to make you obey its passions. Do not present your members to sin as instruments for unrighteousness, but present yourselves to God as those who have been brought from death to life, and your members to God as instruments for righteousness" (Romans 6:12-13). Jesus has freed us from the power of sin so we can serve God's purposes.

Surrender to God's Spirit

In chapter 2, we looked at several examples of how God used weak but willing people as instruments of his grace in the world. God calls us into a relationship with Himself and empowers us to accomplish his purposes on Earth. We become instruments of God's grace in the world as we recognize God's calling to abandon our selfish ambitions and pursue God's will. We are able to pursue God's will because he has given us his Spirit to help us overcome our sin and the desires of our flesh.

The prophet Ezekiel expressed God's frustration with Israel because of their disobedience. Repeatedly, the nation of Israel failed to keep God's commandments. They worshiped the gods of foreign nations and looked after their own self-interests. Israel was supposed to reflect God's character in the world. Instead, they disrespected God by worshiping idols.

God promised to restore his reputation by giving his people the ability to obey his commandments. God said, "I will give you a new heart, and a new spirit I will put within you. And I will remove the heart of stone from your flesh and give you a heart of flesh. And I will put my Spirit within you, and cause you to walk in my statutes and be careful to obey my rules" (Ezekiel 36:26-27).

Israel's sinful nature prevented them from doing God's will. They didn't need a reminder of what was right and what was wrong. They needed a new heart and a new spirit. They needed the power of God to overcome the weakness of their sinful flesh.

The apostle Paul described our sinful desires as the desires of our flesh, which are always in conflict with the desires of God's Spirit. "For the desires of the flesh are against the Spirit, and the desires of the Spirit are against the flesh, for these are opposed to each other, to keep you from doing the things you want to do" (Galatians 5:16).

Apart from our relationship with God, we are utterly helpless to do God's will. We are like the nation of Israel who understood God's law but were not able to accomplish it in their own strength. We need God to accomplish his purposes through us, empowering us to do his will by surrendering ourselves to the Holy Spirit.

The apostle Paul offers the church hope when he says, "Walk by the Spirit, and you will not gratify the desires of the flesh" (Galatians 5:17). God promises to empower his people, giving them the ability to do what was previously impossible: to uphold his commandments before the nations. God, himself, will accomplish his purposes through us, by taking our hearts of stone and giving us a heart of flesh (Ezek 36:26). A spiritually hardened heart is incapable of receiving God's grace, but God promises to give us a new heart that is able to receive God's grace and to reflect his love.

In his letter to Titus, the apostle Paul instructs the church in Crete "to be obedient, to be ready for every good work" (Titus 3:1). He reminds the church of the sinful nature that once kept them captive. "For we ourselves were once foolish, disobedient, led astray, slaves to various passions and pleasures, passing our days in malice and envy, hated by others and hating one another" (Titus 3:2).

Like the Israelites of Ezekiel's day, the people of Crete had been taken captive by their sinful nature. Before their conversion to Christ, the fruitfulness of their lives had been foolishness and disobedience. But God kept his promise to act on their behalf. He freed them from their slavery to their passions and desires. Paul reminded the church of the salvation they had received through Jesus. "He saved us, not because of work done by us in righteousness, but according to his own mercy, by the washing of regeneration and renewal of the Holy Spirit, whom he poured out on us richly through Jesus Christ our Savior" (Titus 3:5-6).

Paul contrasts the weakness of our sinful flesh with the power of God's Spirit to accomplish his purposes through us. In the corruption of our sinful flesh, we are incapable of pleasing God. The law of God magnifies our brokenness and our need for a savior. It highlights our inability to keep God's commands in our own strength. "For while we were living in the flesh, our sinful passions, aroused by the law, were at work in our members to bear fruit for death" (Romans 7:5). But by God's mercy and grace, he accomplishes in us what we were never able to accomplish on our own.

Jesus saves us from the dominion of sin, a power that once forced us into perpetual disobedience. By placing his Spirit within us, God gives us a renewed opportunity to obey him. Disobedience to God is no longer a foregone conclusion. By submitting to the Spirit of God that now lives within us, we are able to carry out good works that honor and glorify God. We are able to obey God, not as a precursor to salvation, but as evidence of the grace of God that is at work within us.

At the conclusion of Paul's gospel presentation in Titus, he encourages Titus to provoke the church to good deeds. "I want you to insist on these things, so that those who have believed in God may be careful to devote themselves to good works" (Titus 3:8). The Spirit of God is now at work within his people, helping them to accomplish his purposes and to bring Him glory.

God will accomplish his purposes through his church. As we learn to submit to the leading of the Holy Spirit, God will overcome our sin, our fears and the desires of our flesh. Our obedience will demonstrate to others the power of God at work within us, just as the scripture promised long ago. "We have this treasure in jars of clay, to show that the surpassing power belongs to God and not to us" (2 Corinthians 4:7).

The Joy of Obedience

My conversation with Mario taught me what Paul meant when he said, "Walk by the Spirit and you will not gratify the desires of your flesh." God used Mario and Tamisha to confront the fear that was preventing me from obeying God. God uprooted my deep-seated fear by using his word in Ezekiel 3:18. As I reflected on the truth of scripture, my fears and sinfulness were revealed. I didn't want to confront Mario because I was scared of what he might do to me. I put my own safety before the safety of my neighborhood. I placed a greater priority on my own well-being than I did on Mario's salvation.

Not only was my attitude toward Mario sinful, but my fears were also misplaced. Mario wasn't the man I made him out to be in my mind. He was gentle, kind, and open to the Spirit of God. God used the passage in Ezekiel to confront my own sinfulness and to provoke me to obedience. As I stepped out in faith, I began to see Mario through the eyes of Christ, as a man in need of God's grace and redemption. In that way, Mario was no different than me. We were both in need of God's grace.

As I reflected on God's word, the Holy Spirit gently led me to put his word into action. God used his church to encourage me to be faithful. Both Tim and Eric prayed for me, asking the

Spirit of God to help me. They reminded me of God's promises and encouraged me to put God's word into practice.

As Mario, Tamisha, and I discussed scripture together, I experienced God's peace. The fear I felt moments before was completely gone. I felt genuine love growing in my heart for my neighbors. I wanted God's best for them. After we prayed together, I walked home feeling overwhelmed by the joy of the Lord. I could feel his pleasure. There were no signs of the consternation that plagued me earlier that day. I felt like I was floating on a cloud. God was pleased with me and I felt his joy.

Psalm 37:4 says, "Delight yourself in the Lord and he will give you the desires of your heart." If you had asked me what I wanted before confronting Mario, I would have said comfort and safety. Those were the desires of my flesh. But if you asked me at the end of the day, after confronting Mario, what was my desire? I would have said I wanted more joy in my life. Joy was the desire of the Spirit, and it was deeply satisfying to me. The joy of obedience is a greater pleasure to me than the desire for comfort. I just wasn't aware of it until after I had surrendered to the leading of the Holy Spirit. Having experienced the joy of the Lord, I can't imagine anything more satisfying. Love, peace, and joy (the fruit of the Spirit) fulfill our desires to a much greater degree than comfort and safety. God created us to share in his joy. When we delight ourselves in God, obeying Him is a joyful experience.

Several years ago, Resurrection Health, one of the Christian healthcare organizations that I worked for, opened a new clinic on the north side of our city. Our staff hosted an open house to meet the residents of the community. My wife, Kim, and I were both in attendance. I was talking to one of the nurses from our clinic when I heard Kim scream. I looked up to see her bolting across the room. When I reached her, she was hugging Mario, Tamisha, and their two children. We hadn't seen them in nearly twelve years.

Mario and Tamisha had gotten married and were raising their two children in a house a couple of blocks from the clinic. It didn't take long for us to reconnect. God gave Kim and me an opportunity to see the fruitfulness of the spiritual seeds that had been planted years ago. Mario and Tamisha were both committed Christians and thriving in their faith. Mario was a worship leader in his church. God was using his testimony to draw other people to Christ.

Kim and I don't often have the opportunity to see the fruit of our labor, but the Spirit of God is constantly working in the hearts of his people, nonetheless. We never know where simple acts of obedience might lead. We were thankful for the opportunity to share in God's joy over the redemption of Mario's family.

Obey the Great Commission

As followers of Jesus, the Spirit of God lives in us, empowering us to obey his commands. God desires to express Himself—his love, his peace, and his joy—through us as we surrender to the leading of his Spirit. God's kingdom breaks into our world every time our fears are extinguished, and our faith is expressed in obedience to Christ. When we obey Jesus, he is glorified, and the world catches a clearer glimpse of the marvelous wonders of his Kingdom.

God will help you to overcome the fears that hinder you from accomplishing God's mission in the world. After his resurrection, Jesus entrusted his disciples with a mission: to make disciples of all nations, teaching them to obey all he commanded (Matthew 28:18-19).

In the chapters that follow, we will explore Jesus' commandments in more depth: to love, to practice hospitality, to be generous, and to forgive. By obeying Jesus' teachings, we invite God's kingdom to come and his will to be done on earth as it is in heaven. The following chapters will paint a clearer picture of what it looks like to be a disciple of Jesus in today's society. I urge you to use the lessons that follow to make disciples of all nations.

In preparation, I ask that you take some time to reflect on Jesus' commission to his church. I encourage you to read Matthew 28:18-20 out loud every day for a week. What is preventing you from teaching others to obey Jesus? Write down the fears you have and ask God to help you overcome them. Share your list with a trusted friend or family member and ask them to pray for you. After asking God to help you obey his command to make disciples of all nations, step out in faith. Reach out to someone of a different nationality than yours. If you don't know anyone, consider volunteering with a local refugee resettlement agency, sharing God's love with the people you meet. Your flesh will resist. Fight through it. Surrender to the leading of the Holy Spirit, and you will experience the joy of the Lord.

Questions for Reflection

1. What is preventing you from obeying Jesus' command to make disciples of all nations?
2. What passage of scripture speaks to your problem?
3. Spend time in prayer. Ask God to give you the grace you need to confront the obstacles you face. Check in with a trusted friend after a week of prayer and update him or her on how you are progressing in obedience.

CHAPTER 5

LIVE BY FAITH AND NOT BY FEAR

"Today, if you hear his voice, do not harden your hearts as in the rebellion."
Hebrews 3:15

Kim and I had been living in our inner-city neighborhood for a couple of months when we were invited to attend a luncheon about the value of relocation for urban ministry. Our move had been stressful. We regularly heard gunshots at night and were struggling with fear. We needed the counsel of a seasoned urban minister to help us regain perspective on why we had chosen to relocate to an impoverished community.

The keynote speaker for the luncheon was Bob Lupton, founder of FCS Ministries in Atlanta, GA. Bob was a long-time board member of the Christian Community Development Association (CCDA) and the author of *Toxic Charity*. Kim and I had spoken with Bob on a couple of occasions and were looking forward to hearing from him again.

We were blessed as Bob recounted the benefits of relocation. He reminded us that we are better able to understand the problems facing the poor when we live together. "Their" problems become "our" problems. Shared experiences build empathy, understanding, and community. By pursuing our desires for safety, quality education, and social advancement in cooperation with our neighbors, we were loving our neighbors as ourselves.

Bob reminded us that God himself relocated from heaven to earth. "The Word became flesh and made his dwelling among us" (John 1:14, NIV). Jesus experienced our problems but was not consumed by them. Jesus was our source of comfort when things went bad. "For we do not have a high priest who is unable to sympathize with our weaknesses, but one who in every respect has been tempted as we are, yet without sin. Let us then with confidence draw near to the throne of grace, that we may receive mercy and find grace to help in time of need" (Hebrews 4:15). As we reflected on the Biblical principles Bob shared, our fears began to subside.

At the end of the meeting, Bob took the time to answer a few questions from the audience. A woman at a table across from us raised her hand. She said, "Bob, I am a single mother with two young children. For years I have felt God leading me to relocate to an inner-city community, but I fear for my children's safety. I don't want to put them in harm's way. Will you please tell me what I should do? Do you have any advice for me?"

If Bob responded to her, I don't remember it. What I remember was a long, awkward silence. My heart broke for the woman. I wanted to console her, but I couldn't find any words of encouragement. I left the luncheon feeling uncomfortable that she had not received the guidance she desired.

Several days later, a friend of mine asked me to teach his Sunday school class. They were studying the book of Hebrews. As I prepared to teach his class, I found the words of encouragement I was looking for.

Fear Opposes Faith

Fear prevents us from following Jesus whole-heartedly. Cowardice prevents people from taking risks and facing danger for the sake of God's Kingdom. Cowardly behavior on the part of God's people protects our self-interests while opposing the interests of God. By placing our faith in Jesus and meditating on the truth of scripture, we can overcome the fears that hinder our obedience to God.

The book of Hebrews was written to Jewish Christians in the first century encouraging them not to recant their faith. They were most likely facing persecution for their beliefs and being pressured to abandon their faith in Jesus. Three times in Hebrews chapters 3-4, the author reminds his audience, "Today if you hear my voice, do not harden your hearts as in the days of rebellion in the wilderness" (Hebrews 3:7-11, 3:15, 4:7). The quote refers to the story of Israel's rebellion in Numbers 13-14, where the Israelites refused to enter the land of Canaan because of their fear.

God was leading his people into the Promised Land, a prosperous land "flowing with milk and honey" (Numbers 13:27). God promised He would give the land to the Israelites (Numbers 13:2). But when the people of Israel saw the land for themselves, they were confronted with a problem. There were Canaanite warriors living on the land whom they feared (Numbers 13:31-33). Would the Israelites maintain faith in God's promise to deliver them from their enemies, or would they abandon God's plan to pursue their own? Would their fear outweigh their faith?

Several times, the Israelites expressed their fears to one another. "The people who live there are powerful, and the cities are fortified and very large" (Numbers 13:28). "The land we explored devours those living in it" (Numbers 13:32). "We seemed like grasshoppers in our own eyes, and we looked the same to them" (Numbers 13:33). As the Israelites measured their own limitations against the size and strength of the Canaanite army, fear grew in their hearts.

They began to grumble and complain against God and his chosen leaders. Their fears grew, climaxing in an act of rebellion. "Why is the Lord bringing us to this land only to let us fall by the sword? Our wives and children will be taken as plunder. Wouldn't it be better for us to go back to Egypt?" (Numbers 14:2-4).

The men of Israel rationalized their disobedience to God. They loved their families and wanted to them from the violence in Canaan. So, they abandoned the mission of God and refused to enter Canaan. Why would God put the women and children of Israel in harm's way? Weren't the men right to protect their families?

The Israelites' fear flowed from their anxious thoughts about the Canaanite armies. As the Israelites meditated on the problems they faced, their fears grew. They reflected on the size of the Canaanite army and on their own limited resources. They didn't think about God. They forgot that God had delivered them from slavery by sending plagues on Egypt. They forgot that God had parted the Red Sea so they could escape from the Egyptian armies. They forgot their praise of God's deliverance, "Your right hand, Lord, was majestic in power. Your right hand, Lord, shattered the enemy" (Exodus 15:6). They allowed their fears to overwhelm their faith in God. Egypt, the place where they were once enslaved, became a place of safety and security for them. The Israelites allowed their thinking to become completely distorted by their fears.

Fear can lead us to abandon our faith in God. The Israelites rebelled against God because they stopped trusting in Him for their salvation. They stopped believing that God would deliver them from their enemies. The author of Hebrews uses their example to warn the Jewish Christians of his day not to make the same mistake. "See to it, brothers and sisters, that none of you has a sinful, unbelieving heart that turns away from the living God" (Hebrews 3:12). We must stand against fears that distort our faith leading to sin and disobedience.

Overcoming Fear with Faith

As Christians, the best thing we can do for our families is to demonstrate how to overcome fear with faith. To maintain faith in the face of fear, our thoughts must be grounded in the truth of scripture. We can be led astray by our own fears and personal convictions of what is right and wrong. Our convictions must be shaped by God's word. When we choose for ourselves what is good and evil instead of listening to God, we are repeating the sin of Adam and Eve. God's will should not be a mystery to us. It is readily available through the Bible. But it takes effort on our part to listen to God's word and to remember his faithfulness. We overcome fear by placing our faith in God's word, trusting that he will accomplish what he promises through the scriptures.

The author of Hebrews compares God's word to a knife that performs surgery on our unbelieving hearts. "For the word of God is alive and active. Sharper than any double-edged sword, it penetrates even to dividing soul and spirit, joints and marrow; it judges the thoughts and attitudes of the heart" (Hebrews 4:12). Reflecting on God's word will uproot the fears of our hearts and uncover our need for faith.

As the people of Israel rebelled against God in the wilderness, two men offered a faithful counter-narrative to the fears of the Israelites. Caleb encouraged the people of God to occupy the land saying, "For we are well able to overcome it" (Numbers 13:30). The Israelites discounted Caleb's word of encouragement and continued to cry out against God. Once again, Caleb and Joshua spoke up, reminding the people of God's faithfulness. "If the Lord delights in us, he will bring us into this land and give it to us, a land that flows with milk and honey. Only do not rebel against the Lord. And do not fear the people of the land, for they are bread for us. Their protection is removed from them, and the Lord is with us; do not fear them" (Numbers 14:8-9). Caleb and Joshua fought fear with faith. They reminded the Israelites of God's promises. God was on their side, and he promised to deliver them.

The Bible is full of verses reminding us to counteract fear with faith. "When I am afraid, I put my trust in you. In God, whose word I praise, in God I trust; I shall not be afraid. What can flesh do to me?" (Psalms 56:3-4). Compared to the all-surpassing power of God, what significance is human opposition? "And do not fear those who kill the body but cannot kill the soul. Rather fear him who can destroy both soul and body in hell" (Matthew 10:28). God alone grants eternal life. Our faith in Jesus ensures that we will live with God forever. Compared to the assurance of our eternal salvation, what is the significance of momentary affliction in this life? Meditating on promises like these in scripture emboldens our faith and diminishes our fears.

After teaching my friend's Sunday school class on the book of Hebrews, God gave me words to share with the single mom at the CCDA luncheon. If I saw her today, I would tell her, "Don't make the same mistake as the Israelites did. Don't use the safety of your children as a justification for disobedience to the Lord's leading. One of the greatest blessings you can offer your children is to model for them how to live by faith and not by fear. God's grace is sufficient for you. You can trust in his plan."

Learning from the Heroes of Our Faith

Everyone has wrestled with fear like the woman at the CCDA luncheon. The Bible is filled with stories of God calling his people to disregard the wisdom of the world to advance God's purposes by faith. The author of Hebrews recounts a list of people who confronted the cultural norms of their day by placing their faith in God. Noah chose to fear God rather than fearing his fellow man. In faith, Noah obeyed God's command to build an ark to escape the torrential floods that were coming. He became an example of those who are saved by faith. "By faith Noah, being warned by God concerning events as yet unseen, in reverent fear constructed an ark for the saving of his household. By this, he condemned the world and became an heir of the righteousness that comes by faith" (Hebrews 11:7).

Abraham became an example of faith for thousands of Christian missionaries who have forsaken home and family to serve God's purposes in a foreign land. "By faith, Abraham obeyed when he was called to go out to a place that he was to receive as an inheritance. And he went out, not knowing where he was going" (Hebrews 11:7-8).

Moses is an example of counter-cultural faith. He resisted the lure of wealth and power to serve God's purposes despite the consequences his obedience would bring. "By faith Moses, when he was grown up, refused to be called the son of Pharaoh's daughter, choosing rather to be mistreated with the people of God than to enjoy the fleeting pleasures of sin" (Hebrews 11:24-25).

The author of Hebrews retells these stories of faithful men to build the faith of his own community. He encourages his community to remember their faithfulness to provoke their own obedience. "Therefore, since we are surrounded by so great a cloud of witnesses, let us also lay aside every weight, and sin which clings so closely, and let us run with endurance the race that is set before us" (Hebrews 12:1).

John and Vera Mae Perkins are two of my spiritual heroes. Their lives of faith have shaped our ministry and given us a model to emulate. John is the visionary leader of the Christian Community Development Association and the Christian Community Health Fellowship, two ministries that have made a profound impact on our lives.

When John was a young man growing up in rural Mississippi, he watched his older brother get shot by a white policeman outside of a pharmacy in his hometown of Mendenhall. John's brother died in his arms as friends raced them to the closest hospital in Jackson, Mississippi. Fearing that John would retaliate for the murder of his brother, a family member suggested that he move to California to live with relatives there.

After he left Mississippi, John's life began to prosper. New economic opportunities that were unavailable to him as a black man living under Jim Crow policies in the South were now available. In addition to new work opportunities, John began to grow and thrive in his faith.

Realizing that he had gifts in evangelism, his church asked him to start a prison ministry. John discovered that he was a natural leader. In addition to his ministry efforts at the prison, he began to learn about economic development, housing co-ops, and other innovative ways to help impoverished communities flourish.

John felt a calling to return to Mississippi to share what he had learned, but his wife Vera Mae was not happy about the prospect of moving back to the South. Their family was growing. They were doing well financially, and they were engaged in meaningful ministry. She questioned why God would send them back to the dangers that awaited them in Mississippi.

Vera Mae began to wrestle with the Lord in prayer. She prayed, "Lord it is not my will to go back to Mississippi, but if it is your will, then change my heart." In time, God answered her prayers. John and Vera Mae relocated to Mississippi and began to minister to their neighbors.

One of their first endeavors was to open a Christian clinic in their hometown of Mendenhall. To recruit a physician, John and Vera Mae networked with doctors at Lawndale Christian Clinic in Chicago. In turn, these doctors coached a couple of young physicians in Memphis through their startup of Christ Community Health Services. Over the years, Christ Community has trained dozens of men and women to start new Christian clinics in urban communities throughout the country. God used Vera Mae's simple prayer of faith to start a movement in the medical community. Clinics in the Christian Community Health Fellowship have served the poor in the name of Christ for more than 50 years.

Vera Mae overcame her fear of returning to Mississippi with faith in God's word. Jesus said, "Truly, truly I say to you unless a grain of wheat falls into the earth and dies it remains alone, but if it dies it bears much fruit. Whoever loves his life loses it, and whoever hates his life in this world will keep it for eternal life. If anyone serves me, he must follow me and where I am, there my servant will be also. If anyone serves me, the Father will honor him" (John 12:24-27).

Jesus' analogy of a seed dying to produce new life was more than a prophecy of his own death and resurrection; it was also an invitation for our own surrender. All who follow Jesus must die to themselves, to their desires for the pleasures and comforts of this world, so that God's purposes might be accomplished on earth through their faith and obedience.

Jesus confronted the corruption of the world. Instead of receiving praise for his good works, he was crucified for them. Spiritual powers of darkness are opposed to Jesus and his church. We will be met with resistance as we seek to serve Jesus and follow in his footsteps, but God has a plan for the prosperity and security of his people. The seeds of suffering that we endure in this life will blossom into honor bestowed on us by God in the last days.

Vera Mae embodied Jesus' teaching on sacrifice and surrender. Her sacrifice to return to Mississippi not only resulted in the establishment of a Christian clinic in her own hometown, but through the relationships that developed since her point of surrender, the Christian Community Health Fellowship has helped hundreds of clinics across the country. Who knows what would have happened if John and Vera Mae had remained in California. But because of Vera Mae's faithfulness to die to herself, millions of people have received healthcare in the name of Christ. Jesus' words were modeled in Vera Mae's life, "If a seed falls to the ground and dies it bears much fruit."

John Perkins is lauded as a visionary leader. He is a great man of God, but Vera Mae is the unsung hero who grounded their ministry in faith. I have witnessed firsthand the protective love of a wife and mother through my wife Kim. I know the fierce loyalty she has for our children and for me. To place a family's well-being in the hands of God, exposing it to the threat of racism and violence, takes an incredible act of faith on the part of a mother.

Vera Mae's example of obedience has been repeated thousands of times by faithful women who have entrusted the care of their families to God. The sacrifices of these women serve a greater purpose than securing the well-being of their families. It is only through the sacrificial love of Jesus and his church that neighborhoods and nations will experience the peace of God. At times, God tells us to lay aside what we believe is in the best interest of our families to pursue what is in the best interest of God's mission to the world.

Applying Our Faith to God's Mission

After the CCDA luncheon with Bob Lupton, my wife and I decided to name our first son Caleb as a reminder to live by faith in the promises of God. When Caleb was eighty years old, he was honored by God for the faith he demonstrated in the wilderness. He was one of only two men, the other being Joshua, who entered the land of Canaan forty years after Israel's rebellion.

As they entered Canaan to receive their inheritance, Caleb in his old age remembered God's promise to give him the land. He made a pledge to the Lord saying, "I am as strong today as I was in my youth...It may be that the Lord will be with me, and I shall drive out [the giants] just as the Lord said" (Joshua 14:11-12). Caleb's faith never wavered. He was just as willing to join God in battle at age eighty as he was at age forty. I pray that God will honor you in the same way he honored Caleb. At the end of your life, I pray that you will stand in the presence of the Lord in eager anticipation of receiving your inheritance because, by God's grace, you lived by faith and not by fear.

Until that day comes, the church has work to do. We have not yet completed the task that Jesus has given us. When the disciples asked Jesus when his Kingdom would come, Jesus said, "This gospel of the kingdom will be proclaimed throughout the whole world as a testimony to all nations, and then the end will come" (Matthew 24:14). The nations in the greatest need of Jesus' gospel are also the most hostile to it. These countries are often politically unstable, religiously intolerant, and opposed to missionary service. They are countries where Christians are martyred for their faith. Despite the obstacles we face, we can't let our fears prevent us from fulfilling God's mission.

The apostle Paul said, "Faith comes from hearing, and hearing through the word of Christ" (Romans 10:17). If we want to grow in our faith and follow Jesus' footsteps, we must put our fears to death by listening to the truth of scripture. If we truly listen to God's word, our faith will grow. By God's grace, we will have the strength to reshape our priorities and our commitments. As we flood our minds with the truth of scripture, the values of the world will lose their grip on us, and we will experience greater freedom to follow Jesus to the ends of the earth.

I encourage you to take inventory of your fears. What is preventing you from fully surrendering your life to Christ? For each fear on your list, find a verse from scripture that will help you dispel your fears with faith. Write out a statement of faith for your family, committing yourselves to fulfill Jesus' mission in spite of its costs.

Questions for Reflection

1. What are your greatest fears?
2. How do your fears prevent you from following Jesus wholeheartedly?
3. How would your life be different if you lived by faith and not by fear?

CHAPTER 6

SEEK SHALOM

"But seek the welfare of the city where I have sent you into exile, and pray to the Lord on its behalf, for in its welfare you will find your welfare."
Jeremiah 29:7

In 2001, Kim and I felt God leading us to move into an urban neighborhood in Memphis and to raise our family there. I didn't have a clear vocation in mind, but I was certain that we were supposed to live out our faith in community and learn how to love our neighbors, responding to their needs with the gospel of Jesus Christ.

At the time, we were both employed by a large church focused on missions and evangelism. It was the church that I grew up in as a teenager. My faith was solidified in this church. Numerous men and women poured Godly wisdom into my life and taught me what it meant to be a disciple of Jesus. The leaders of the church exposed me to vibrant urban ministries and international church planting. A half-dozen men in the church invested significant time in my life. They helped me to understand God's saving grace, taught me how to read and understand the Bible, modeled sacrificial service, took me on mission trips and gave me opportunities to grow as a Christian leader. I am grateful for the spiritual impact they made on my life.

Over the course of the first few years of living in our new neighborhood, Kim and I began to feel an internal tension. We lived and worked in two different cultures. Our church was white and affluent. CEOs and CFOs of major corporations were our friends, our Sunday School teachers, and our mission partners. Our neighbors were black and living below the poverty line. These two cultures coexisted side by side, but there was very little overlap between the two worlds. None of our neighbors attended our church, and no one in our church lived in our community. Every time we made the ten-minute commute from home to church, it felt like we were teleporting to another planet.

Seventeen years later, it is still difficult to label the emotions we felt at the time. We were consistently around people we loved, yet we felt isolated and alone. We had great relationships in both communities. We felt accepted, affirmed and supported, yet we were broken, unable to bridge the cultural divide we experienced every day.

Our neighborhood was broken, filled with people who had experienced violence and trauma. Our church was broken. People in our church were filled with good intentions, but like us, they had little understanding of how to engage our neighborhood. We moved into our neighborhood to serve God in his mission to reconcile the world to himself, hoping that He would use us to bridge the cultural divide that plagued our city. What we encountered were our own profound weaknesses and cultural ineptitude.

Undefeated was an Academy Award-winning documentary produced in 2012 about a white football coach who volunteered to work at an all-black high school in Memphis. In an interview about the film, the coach recounted a conversation that he had with one of his players. The coach was frustrated that some of his players remained aloof after months of working together. Desiring to win the affection of his football team, he asked one of the students why he wasn't able to connect with the football players in a more meaningful way. The young man was open and honest in his reply. "Coach, they wonder if you're a turkey man."

Dumbfounded, the coach responded, "What is a turkey man?"

"At Thanksgiving and Christmas, people from the suburbs show up in minivans and drop off turkeys, presents and other stuff. We take them because we need them. They seem to be nice people, but they leave, and we never see them again. It makes you wonder after a while if those people are helping because they care about us or if they're doing it to tell people about the nice things they did. We're wondering what you're really about."

Hearing the coach's story was convicting. I felt like a turkey man. A suburban church dropped off dozens of boxes to a local ministry in our neighborhood every holiday season filled with turkeys, canned goods, and small gifts. I was recruited to find families and help distribute the boxes. I was happy to do so at the time. The food baskets were given with a spirit of generosity and were received with gratitude, but they didn't contain what the church, our community, or I desperately needed: mutually beneficial relationships between people of different backgrounds. We needed relationships that restored dignity for a true sense of community to emerge. We needed a different framework to understand how to pursue God's purposes with our neighbors.

The Biblical Basis of God's Shalom

When Kim and I started our ministry in Binghampton, we were urban neophytes. My experience with urban culture was limited to several summers serving as a volunteer for SOS, an urban home repair camp in Memphis. Through those experiences, God gave me a burden for spiritual renewal in our city. But the burden I experienced wasn't accompanied by a plan. I didn't know how to relieve the burden I was experiencing.

Another pastor who had more experience in urban ministry suggested I read Jeremiah's letter to the Israelite refugees in Babylon. Through his letter, the prophet Jeremiah described an approach to the type of urban renewal that our hearts longed for. "Thus says the Lord of hosts, the God of Israel, to all the exiles whom I have sent into exile from Jerusalem to Babylon: Build houses and live in them; plant gardens and eat their produce. Take wives and have sons and daughters; take wives for your sons, and give your daughters in marriage, that they may bear sons and daughters; multiply there, and do not decrease. But seek the welfare of the city where I have sent you into exile, and pray to the Lord on its behalf, for in its welfare you will find your welfare" (Jeremiah 29:4-7).

For hundreds of years, God endured the disobedience of his people as they worshiped false gods, made sacrifices to idols, and treated one another unjustly. God sent prophets to warn his people, telling them to stop their evil practices and to return to Him. When the Israelites refused to repent, God issued a decree. God empowered the pagan Babylon empire to conquer his people and to remove them from the land God had given. God was allowing the Israelites to experience the consequences of their actions.

It is to the Jewish leaders who were taken into exile that Jeremiah addressed his letter. He cautioned them not to resist the Babylonian captivity but to settle in the city, "to build houses and live in them, to plant gardens and eat their produce. To take wives and have sons and daughters." Instead of looking for a way to escape their captivity in Babylon, they were to embrace their new home and to seek the welfare of their oppressors.

Jeremiah tells them to seek the shalom of the city. *Shalom* is the Hebrew word for *peace* but it means more than the absence of conflict. It means completeness or wholeness. Shalom encompasses one's well-being and security. It is a promise of prosperity and blessing. It represents God's intention in creation. It describes the world as it will be when God's purposes are accomplished.

Jeremiah was not telling the people to seek a peaceful resolution to the conflict between Babylon and Israel. The conflict was a result of God's will. The conflict between the two nations was accomplishing God's purposes. The Israelites who were captured and stripped from their homes by a foreign power were commanded by the prophet to seek the well-being of their oppressor—to do what was in the best interest of the pagan community in which they found themselves. They were told to pray for the shalom of Babylon. Together, Babylonians and Israelites alike would experience God's blessing.

The prophet Daniel served as an example of what seeking shalom looked like during the Babylonian exile. He used God's gift of wisdom to bless the kings of Babylon as he served in their courts. In his service to the foreign kings, he never sacrificed his integrity as a servant of God. He continued to worship God even after an edict from the king explicitly forbid his religious practice. The king's courtly officials attempted to rid themselves of Daniel by throwing him to the lions in retribution for his defiance of the new law, but God vindicated Daniel by delivering him from death. After witnessing Daniel's deliverance from the lion's den, the king issued a second edict, commanding everyone in the empire to worship Daniel's God.

Through Daniel's faithful witness, God turned the heart of the king and with it a nation. In Babylon's shalom, Daniel found shalom. As the Babylonians recognized God's power and turned to him in worship, Daniel experienced newfound freedom to worship the God he loved. Together, they experienced the world as God intended it, where nations gather together in worship receiving God's grace and blessing.

While the experience of shalom was short-lived for Daniel and the Israelites in Babylon, Daniel's experience was a precursor to the kingdom that is coming through Jesus. Jesus is the Son of Man, who was given authority over every tribe, tongue, and nation on earth (Daniel 7:13). Jesus will usher in God's eternal kingdom where we will find a full and permanent expression of God's shalom.

Jesus established the shalom of God through his crucifixion (Col 1:20), conquering the sin that separates us from God (Rom 5:1), allowing us to experience peace with God and with one another (Ephesians 2:14-15). God establishes his shalom now in our hearts. When we surrender to Christ's authority, we experience his peace (Col 3:15). When the problems of the world seem too much to bear, by setting our mind on the life of God's Spirit (Rom 8:6) and by meditating on God's goodness (Phil 4:8), we experience God's peace.

The shalom of God's kingdom is all-encompassing. Not only does God give us peace through our personal devotion to Him, but God's peace is ever extending to the whole of his creation. We were created to experience God's love through a relationship with Him and with one another. Shalom is a communal experience. Just as Jeremiah instructed the Jewish exiles to find their peace by seeking the well-being of their oppressors, Jesus instructed his church to love their enemies, doing good to one's oppressors, and giving generously to all (Luke 6:27-36). We experience wholeness as Jesus brings healing to our communities, not just to individuals in our community.

Jesus addressed both the plight of the individual and the root causes of brokenness in the community. It is only by addressing both personal and social brokenness that God's shalom is experienced.

Jonathan Brooks is a friend of mine who lives in Inglewood, a neighborhood in South Chicago, and he is seeking God's shalom for his community. He wrote a terrific book called *Church Forsaken.* He argues that there are no God-forsaken places. God's grace is available to all. There are only church-forsaken places, neighborhoods where the church is afraid to engage with the love of God. I recently heard him preach a dynamic sermon on Jesus healing the Gerasene demoniac (Mark 5:1-20).

Jesus delivered the man by casting out a legion of demons. Curiously, the demons begged Jesus to cast them into a large herd of pigs that were feeding on the hillside. Jesus granted their request. Isn't it odd that Jesus would grant the request of a legion of demons? The pigs rushed into the lake and drowned. Gerasene was one of the cities of the Decapolis—ten Gentile cities that lined the eastern bank of the sea of Galilee.

Jonathan made the astute observation that just as the Jews raised sheep for the dual purpose of diet and sacrifice, Gentile swine herders raised pigs to be sacrificed at the Greek temples in the Decapolis. By sending the demons into the swine, Jesus was not only healing the man, but he was also addressing the root cause of a societal sin: false worship of pagan gods.

For society to experience the shalom of God, we need to experience both personal salvation and social justice. Our societal structures must reflect the values of God's kingdom. The same spiritual beings that haunted the demoniac were being honored in the temples of Gerasene. The Gerasene swine herders were profiting from the false worship of the citizens of their city. When they observed Jesus' power to restore the demoniac, they were not grateful for Jesus' miracle. They were upset that their economic security was being taken away from them. They pleaded for Jesus to leave.

Personal and social sins are intricately tied to one another. Personal deliverance should lead to societal change. To experience the shalom God desires, faithful Christians must apply principles of sacrifice, surrender, and obedience in their workplaces, not just in their homes and places of worship.

Challenging Systems of Injustice

Shalom describes the world as it will be when God completes his ministry of reconciling all things together under the authority of Jesus Christ (Colossians 1:9-16). God's shalom puts Christ at the center of his creation. Everything was created by Jesus and for Jesus—every political, economic, and religious system is created to honor Jesus. We experience peace as these systems serve Christ.

As Jesus heals individuals, he also challenges the systems that keep people in bondage. As we have grown in our understanding of the gospel, we are becoming more aware of the need to challenge the root causes of poverty and oppression in our own community. Gospel presentations cannot be limited to pleas for personal salvation. They must also address the root causes of brokenness in politics, the economy, housing, education, and healthcare. To experience God's shalom together, each of these areas of shared communal life must reflect the grace of God. There is no room for pursuing personal benefit at the expense of the community.

Jeremiah's plea to the Israelites in exile provided a point of clarity for Kim and me as we pursued a calling to serve God in our city. Our welfare was now intimately tied to our neighborhood. As we prayed for and sought the welfare of our community, we would find our well-being.

One of the first opportunities we had to serve our community was to volunteer at Club 61, an after-school program run by one of our friends at a local elementary school. We had opportunities to build relationships with about 80 children several days a week, sharing stories from the Bible and administering activities to occupy their time while they waited for their parents to get off work. Our friend did an amazing job of ingratiating herself to the principal and teachers of the school. At times, she served as a volunteer social worker addressing truancies. She also assisted teachers in their classroom and helped administrators with special projects. She was engaged in the school and built deep and lasting relationships with the children in our neighborhood.

But the burden she carried was immense. The school was failing. It was the lowest-performing school in the state of Tennessee. One year, the principal took a medical leave of absence without telling anyone. For the entire spring semester, the school was without a principal. The turnover for teachers and administrators was high. There was a new principal at the school for several years in a row. Many of the children were being traumatized at home, witnessing domestic abuse and community violence. Increased trauma led to behavioral problems and dysfunction in the classroom. There was a general feeling of chaos at the school for many years.

Several years later, when it came time to choose where to send our own children to school, we were faced with a lot of questions. Would we send our children to one of the two elementary schools that served our neighborhood? Would we homeschool our children or send them to one of the private schools in our city? What was in the best interest of our family? What was in the best interest of the community? Were Jeremiah's words applicable to us in this situation? What did it mean to seek the welfare of our city through this particular decision? Could we experience shalom together with our neighbors through the local schools?

We decided to send our son to the public school that we were zoned for. It wasn't the school that Kim and I volunteered with several years before, but it was one of the neighborhood elementary schools. Our son would be going to school with the same children who lived on our street. The experience was better than expected. The shared experience of sending our son to school with our neighbors opened up many new relationships. When he started playing on sports teams with other children in the neighborhood, even more relationships opened to us. We were feeling more a part of the community. The school felt safe, and while the academic standards of the school weren't great, we liked his teachers and were able to provide additional learning opportunities for him at home.

There were plenty of frustrations too. It felt like some of the school administrators were trying to lower expectations rather than working to raise academic standards. New initiatives were frowned upon, and teacher morale was generally low. Many felt overworked and under-supported.

When our son entered the second grade, a new opportunity arose. The other school in our neighborhood, the one with the lowest standardized test scores in the state where Kim and I had volunteered for Club 61, was being converted to a charter school. Friends from the church where I had grown up were helping to lead the new school. A local ministry that trained Christian teachers to raise academic standards in the public school system was providing a steady stream of motivated teachers to the classroom. The new principal had the freedom to start creating new initiatives. It felt like God was answering our prayers for our neighborhood. We were experiencing the first fruits of prospering together with our neighbors.

The first couple of years at the new school brought both positive and negative attention. Arne Duncan, the US Secretary of Education, visited the school to acknowledge the tremendous progress the school had made in advancing test scores and academic standards. But there was also a backlash in the community. People who had graduated from the school in the past did not like some of the changes that were being made. The name of the school was changed. Sports programs that were a source of community pride were dropped to make more time for educational training. Some residents felt that the new disciplinary tactics were overbearing and culturally insensitive. Others in the community complained that their voice wasn't being heard and that some of the changes that were being made alienated them. They felt marginalized from their own school.

It was a tremendous learning experience for both the school and our family. The experience reiterated the necessity of working together with the community, not for the community. The school administrators listened and made adjustments, adding community leaders to its board, and changing some of their practices to be more inclusive of the community.

For Kim and me, it has been a long process of learning to let go of our desire for control and to pursue a shared agenda for our community. But looking back, we could see that we were several steps closer to experiencing the fullness of God's shalom. We don't pass out turkey boxes anymore. Friends from my home church are investing themselves in the lives of our community. The children that we first met at Club 61 are becoming leaders in our neighborhood. God's shalom is growing, and we are beginning to experience his prosperity together.

Activating the Assets of a Community

Shalom is experienced when everything is put in its rightful place. Where everyone is valued and has an opportunity to use the gifts God has bestowed upon them for the good of the whole community. Looking at the community through the lens of shalom shifted my thinking about our neighborhood. Instead of looking at the neighborhood's deficits, I started looking for its assets. What God-given gifts and abilities did people have in our neighborhood? Were they being invited to share their gifts to improve the well-being of the community?

A couple of years ago, Kim and I gathered several of our neighbors together to discuss the problems facing our neighborhood. Each person was given three sticky notes and instructed to list a problem facing our community on each one. We put the notes on a board and organized them by theme. Next, we had each person vote on the problem they thought posed the greatest threat to our community and ranked them by need. Finally, we asked each person if they wanted to be involved in providing a solution to the problems we faced as a community.

The three biggest concerns were improving the safety of our neighborhood, helping women to escape sex trafficking, and helping men with felonies to find meaningful employment. Our neighbor Johnny had been a security officer in his younger days. He organized a neighborhood meeting with our city councilman and advocated for the city to install security cameras on our street.

A woman in our neighborhood had escaped prostitution and wanted to help other women do the same. She started a drop-in center with the support of a neighborhood church so women could get off the street and have a safe place to shower, eat, and wash their clothes. Our ministry purchased a home for men to live in while they transitioned from prison to self-sufficiency. Each of us used the gifts God had given us to work for the mutual benefit of our community.

Unfortunately, our schools, our healthcare system, and our criminal justice system still suffer from deep-seated problems and inequalities. We live in a two-tiered society where those with resources receive a better education, better healthcare, and better opportunities to raise their families in safe environments. As men and women surrender their lives to Jesus, seeking the shalom of their communities, the world will experience God's love in deep and tangible ways. We need more Christians to engage the systems of the world by entering into them with God's love, using their gifts and influence to create meaningful change.

For Kim and me, engaging our community with God's shalom has involved progressive steps of faith and obedience. I hope that God is tugging at your heart to engage the systems of the world by seeking his shalom. I would encourage you to begin by listening to people in your community who are struggling with the unjust social systems in our society. Kim and I began to get a sense of the problems in our community by volunteering at our local school. You might consider doing the same. You could interview parents of children at a poor performing school in your community. Get an understanding of the problems from their perspective and ask them what they would do to improve the school system.

Talk to a patient at a free and charitable clinic and ask them about the services that are available to them and those that are not. Do they have access to a full range of services to support their mental and physical health? Talk to someone who has been incarcerated and ask them about their experience with the criminal justice system. Did they have a lawyer who listened to them and served their interests? Were they able to pay for bail? How long did they have to wait in jail before receiving a trial?

Next, think about how different your own life experiences have been. I hope this doesn't sound too harsh, but the differences you have experienced are not a result of God's blessing. You have a better education because you had access to better educational opportunities. You have better healthcare because you can pay for better insurance coverage. There are often others, beyond our immediate purview, who do not have access to those same opportunities.

God has not withheld his blessing from those who are poor and marginalized. Because of sin, we are inclined to seek our own self-interests. That means that the social systems we have built for ourselves benefit those with the greatest resources and influence over our political systems. Those with less influence are marginalized. This is a universal truth. Injustices exist in every society because we sinfully seek our own self-interests to the exclusion of others.

The most profound way that Kim and I have found to engage in building a more equitable society is to follow Jeremiah's advice by entering into the broken systems of our world, seeking the mutual benefit of both the oppressor and the oppressed. God is sending his church to storm the gates of Hell by engaging systems of injustice with his love. God desires for all people to experience his blessing, both rich and poor. God bestows his blessing of shalom as we build communities that reflect the values of his kingdom. Will you prayerfully consider how to seek God's shalom in your own community?

Questions for Reflection

1. How have you experienced God's shalom?
2. What is hindering the growth of shalom in the city where you live?
3. How would your life be different if you made important decisions based on what was in the best interest of your community?

CHAPTER 7

HONOR GOD WITH YOUR TITHE

"There will never cease to be poor in the land. Therefore I command you, 'You shall open wide your hand to your brother, to the needy and to the poor.'"
Deuteronomy 15:11

I was pulling out of the driveway when I noticed my neighbor flagging me down. I stopped the truck and got out to speak with him. He was difficult for me to understand. Sometimes, he slurred his words due to a recent stroke. The muffler on my truck was also going out. It was a bad combination. He asked if I could give him a ride to the doctor's office to get his prescription refilled.

"Not now," I said. "I have to go to work."

It was a half-truth. I was on my way to the office, but I had the time and flexibility to take him to the doctor's office if I wanted to. I started to get back into my truck but felt convicted. I knew my neighbor lived alone and was in poor health.

"Can you call your doctor and have him refill the prescription over the phone?" I asked.

"My phone was stolen."

"Do you want to use my phone?"

"No. I need to see my doctor. He won't refill the prescription without a check-up. It will only take five minutes."

I knew better. I had worked for a Christian medical clinic for over a decade. Nothing took five minutes. My neighbor got in my truck, and we drove to his doctor's office. During the ride, he opened up about his health concerns and his family life.

"Why do you need medicine?" I asked.

"I had my colon removed. Want to see the scar?"

He lifted up his shirt to show me a large gash across his stomach. He had a stroke two years before his colon surgery. He was advancing in age and declining in health. I had been to his house on a few occasions, to help him move furniture and find a bottle of medicine he had lost.

After his stroke, he had difficulty getting around. He was a very independent person, but he was getting to a point in life where he needed help from other people. He said he had a daughter who lived in Alabama. I asked if he had considered moving to Alabama so his daughter could take care of him.

"Tried that already. Didn't work."

"What happened?"

"She stole $1,000 from me. She gave it to her boyfriend so he could buy a car. She looks nice on the outside, but she's the devil."

"What about your church? I know you had several church members who came by to check on you after you had your stroke. Do you think any of them could help you now?"

"They burned out."

"What do you mean?"

"They got tired of helping me."

When we arrived at the doctor's office, I dropped my neighbor off at the door. I made a few phone calls outside while I waited for my friend to see his physician. When I went inside the doctor's office, he was still waiting. After an hour of waiting, the receptionist said that his doctor wasn't even in the office that day. My neighbor would need to make another appointment to get his medicine refilled. The next available appointment was in three months.

A Solemn Warning

When people who are trapped in cycles of poverty ask for help, their requests are easily brushed aside. They can become invisible, neglected by family, friends, and even the church. We often lose sight of the poor, but God always sees them. God ensured that the poor would be cared for by establishing provisions for them in his law. When his people failed to uphold his law, God reminded them of their obligation through the prophets.

Caring for the poor is one of the central tenets of Christianity. It is one of the ways that we can storm the gates of Hell, liberating people from bondage. By giving to the poor in their time of need, we liberate them from financial bondage, reflecting God's grace and generosity. Jesus reminded the church to give to the poor. He told the story of a poor man named Lazarus who was neglected by his wealthy neighbor:

> There was a rich man who was clothed in purple and fine linen and who feasted sumptuously every day. And at his gate was laid a poor man named Lazarus, covered with sores, who desired to be fed with what fell from the rich man's table. Moreover, even the dogs came and licked his sores.
>
> The poor man died and was carried by the angels to Abraham's side. The rich man also died and was buried, and in Hades, being in torment, he lifted up his eyes and saw Abraham far off and Lazarus at his side. And he called out, "Father Abraham, have mercy on me, and send Lazarus to dip the end of his finger in water and cool my tongue, for I am in anguish in this flame."

> But Abraham said, "Child, remember that you in your lifetime received your good things, and Lazarus in like manner bad things; but now he is comforted here, and you are in anguish. And besides all this, between us and you, a great chasm has been fixed, in order that those who would pass from here to you may not be able, and none may cross from there to us."
>
> And he said, "Then I beg you, father, to send him to my father's house— for I have five brothers—so that he may warn them, lest they also come into this place of torment." But Abraham said, "They have Moses and the Prophets; let them hear them." And he said, "No, Father Abraham, but if someone goes to them from the dead, they will repent." He said to him, "If they do not hear Moses and the Prophets, neither will they be convinced if someone should rise from the dead." (Luke 16:19-31)

Lazarus was not much to look at. His body was covered in sores. Stray dogs licked his open wounds, providing a kind of salve. It was a poor man's healthcare. Overlooked by those with the power and resources to make a difference in his life, Lazarus waited for mercy but never received it. By the description that was given to him, I imagine Lazarus looked and smelled like poverty. I am sure he inspired both sympathy and repulsion to onlookers, but the rich man was not moved to action. He ignored Lazarus and the moral obligation of his faith to care for him.

Unfortunately, I can identify with the rich man. Although I made an intentional decision to live in a low-income neighborhood, I still build emotional walls around my heart all the time. I find it difficult to engage with people in poverty, to enter into the chaos that many of them suffer through. I'm selfish. I don't want to get mired in the endless layers of dysfunction that envelop the poor. I long for a sense of accomplishment in my work, but laboring with the poor doesn't always produce positive outcomes. I often get swept up into their despair, rather than giving the hope I have in Christ. When I encounter a request for help, I have to decide: am I going to take down the emotional wall I have built for myself and engage, or am I going to absolve myself of responsibility to the poor by upholding my scheduled commitments with the affluent?

Many of us find the proximity of poverty and its accompanying problems too much to bear, moving into gated communities to assuage our fears. Is there a problem with that? Is it wrong to escape the cares of the world, seeking more stability for ourselves and our families? Protecting my children from the threats of the world seems responsible, not sinful. But in doing so, I need to ask myself, am I pursuing a lifestyle of my own choosing, or am I following Christ? Am I repeating the sins of Adam and Eve, choosing for myself what is right and wrong, instead of relying upon God for his direction? Am I willing to choose the hard path, following the lessons of my faith, embracing a kingdom built around an ethic of love and mercy? Will I have the courage to seek God's kingdom instead of pursuing self-interests to the exclusion of others?

The Purpose of the Tithe

The dramatic nature of the rich man's consequence, suffering torment in hell for neglecting the poor man at his gate, is intended to direct our attention to Abraham's warning: listen to Moses and the prophets. God has already given us instructions for caring for the poor. We should listen intently to God's warning.

The Jewish law, or Torah, was comprised of the first five books of the Old Testament. In Deuteronomy 14-15, the fifth book in the Torah, Moses instructs the people of Israel to care for the poor. Moses begins his teaching on the poor by telling the Israelites to set aside a tithe, or a tenth of their income, every year. Tithing is still practiced by many churches today, although the connection to the original purpose of the tithe in Deuteronomy 14:22-29 has been lost.

I have never heard anyone teach on the Biblical purpose of the tithe from the passage in Deuteronomy. I wish more pastors would. It would change the way we practice our Christian faith, and it would positively influence the way our faith is perceived by others. The rich man in Jesus' story seems to have forgotten the purpose of the tithe as well. It behooves us to revisit God's instruction through the law and the prophets, to better understand the reformation Jesus hopes to bring by telling the story of the rich man and Lazarus.

The main purpose of the tithe was to teach the people of Israel to fear the Lord (Deuteronomy 14:23). Israel lived in an agrarian economy. Their wealth was produced by managing the land God entrusted to them. The land belonged to the Lord (Leviticus 25:23). God tended to it, ensuring its fertility (Deuteronomy 11:12). In a sense, the Israelites were God's vassals, tenants who tended to the land God owned. In exchange for honoring God by keeping his law, God promised to provide for his people.

The word *tithe* means "a tenth." The Israelites were expected to set aside a tenth of the produce from their crops each year. The tithe was to be consumed by the people of Israel, "in the place that God will choose to make his name dwell" (Deuteronomy 14:23). This phrase is repeated throughout the book of Deuteronomy (12:5, 11, 21; 16:2, 6, 11; 26:2) and most likely refers to the tabernacle, which moved about from place to place as the Israelites migrated through the wilderness and the land of Canaan. Later in Israel's history, King Solomon built the Temple in Jerusalem as a "house for the name of the Lord" (1 Kings 8:20).

Moses instructed the people of Israel to take their tithe to the place of worship (the tabernacle and later the Temple), but instead of using the tithe to make an offering to the Lord, Moses instructed the Israelites to consume it in God's presence. "You shall eat the tithe of your grain, of your wine, and of your oil, and the firstborn of your herd and flock" (Deuteronomy 14:23). If it was too much of a burden to carry a tenth of their crops from their farmland to the tabernacle, Moses told the Israelites to exchange their crops for money before making the journey. When they arrived "at the place God had chosen to make his name known," they were to "spend the money for whatever you desire—oxen or sheep or wine or strong drink, whatever your appetite craves" (Deuteronomy 14:26).

I don't know about you, but this concept of the tithe was never explained to me. It sounds a lot more fun than passing a plate around during a church service. God taught the Israelites to fear his name by commanding them to enjoy a feast with their tithe! Each year, the harvest was a reminder of God's faithfulness to provide for his people. God demonstrated his grace by giving back to the Israelites what rightfully belonged to him.

The tithe wasn't used for church programs, building campaigns, or pastor's salaries. It wasn't used for church retreats, evangelism outreach, or youth events. And, at least at this point in the narrative, it wasn't even used for relief and development work. God wanted his people to trust him. The celebration of the tithe was a time to rejoice in the goodness of God.

The tithe is one of the first pictures we have in the Bible of what the kingdom of God will be like. It was a precursor to Jesus' parables, where Jesus describes God's kingdom as a great banquet. In Luke 14:15-24, while Jesus shared a meal with a prominent Pharisee and his friends, he reminded the religious leaders that the kingdom of God will be like a great party, where everyone is invited to share in God's grace. Jesus warned his audience not to get caught up in the cares of this world by focusing on their jobs, their investments or their family obligations thereby missing out on the celebratory community that God was bringing together.

The rich man didn't invite Lazarus to join his party. Lazarus was left to observe the festivities of the rich man's banquet from the wrong side of the rich man's gate. The banquet of the rich man was the exact opposite of God's kingdom. It was a worldly celebration that ignored the presence of the poor. Jesus encouraged his followers to incorporate the poor into their celebrations. He said, "When you give a luncheon or dinner, do not invite your friends, your brothers or sisters, your relatives, or your rich neighbors; if you do, they may invite you back and so you will be repaid. But when you give a banquet, invite the poor, the crippled, the lame, the blind, and you will be blessed. Although they cannot repay you, you will be repaid at the resurrection of the righteous" (Luke 14:12-14).

The tithe also involved a direct command to care for the poor. Every third year, God instructed the Israelites to give their tithe to the Levites, widows, orphans, and foreigners in the land instead of bringing it to the tabernacle. These four groups of people did not have access to the means of production in Israel's agrarian economy. God provided for them through the generosity of his people. The Israelites gave their tithe to Levites living in their cities. The Levites were allowed to keep a portion of the tithe for themselves, but they were also responsible for storing it and redistributing it to the vulnerable as they had need of it.

The Role of the Prophets

Throughout the history of Israel, religious leaders became selfish and broke God's commandment regarding the tithe. They provided for themselves with the tithe but excluded the poor. Instead of sharing the tithe with the poor, they hoarded it for themselves. The prophets called for repentance, warning of God's judgment if they persisted in their selfishness and disobedience.

In Ezekiel 34:2-3, the prophet issued a warning to Israel's leaders saying, "Woe to you shepherds of Israel who only take care of yourselves! Should not shepherds take care of the flock? You eat the curds, clothe yourselves with the wool and slaughter the choice animals, but you do not take care of the flock." The religious leaders of Israel were misusing their authority by providing an extravagant lifestyle for themselves at the expense of the poor. Instead of sharing the tithe with those in need, they hoarded it for themselves.

Malachi issued a similar warning to every Israelite, not just its leaders. "Bring the whole tithe into the storehouse, that there may be food in my house" (Malachi 3:10). In this case, the Israelites were withholding their tithe, again presumably to care for their own needs instead of filling the storehouses with food that could be redistributed to the poor. God attempted to dispel the fear that was driving them to selfishness by promising to bless them and to provide for their needs as they meet the needs of the poor through the tithe.

Luke also addresses the selfish misappropriation of the tithe by the religious leaders of his day. In Luke 20:46-47, Jesus warned people about the scribes who seek to raise their status and enhance their lifestyle, again at the expense of the poor. They "like to walk around in long robes, and love greetings in the marketplaces and the best seats in the synagogues and the places of honor at feasts," all while "devouring widows' homes."

In the very next passage, Jesus tells the story of a widow who gave her entire livelihood to the temple treasury. While it is true that Jesus honored this woman for her generosity, he also shamed the religious leaders for their hypocrisy. If the religious leaders were adhering to the law, they would have redistributed the tithe to the widow, caring for her in her time of need. Instead, her contribution to the temple was misappropriated and used to enhance the status of the scribes, paying for their luxurious lifestyle. The reader of Luke's gospel is given an immediate example of how the scribes "devour widows' homes" by taking all that the widow had to live on without giving anything in return.

Today, we are in danger of repeating the sins of our past. Pastors continue to teach their constituents to give generously to the church, promising that God will bless them if they do. But are we consistently redistributing God's resources to the poor? Are we still enhancing pastors' lifestyles to the exclusion of the poor? Will the poor receive God's intended blessing through our tithes and offerings?

In the book of Acts, Luke gives us a couple of positive examples of how the early church was faithful to the spirit of the tithe in Deuteronomy 14. The early church's witness serves as a model for us today. After being filled by the Spirit, the early Christians had the capacity to resist the temptation of selfishness. They demonstrated their newfound grace by generously sharing with others. "And all who believed were together and had all things in common. And they were selling their possessions and belongings and distributing the proceeds to all, as any had need" (Acts 2:44-45). We even see signs of the celebratory meal found in Deuteronomy. "Day by day, attending the temple together and breaking bread in their homes, they received their food with glad and generous hearts, praising God and having favor with all the people" (Acts 2:46-47).

The church's faithfulness was a sign that God's kingdom was coming. The people of God upheld his commandments through the power of the Holy Spirit. They surrendered their lives to Jesus. They loved God and their neighbors. Having received God's grace, they generously shared all they had with one another. God was honored, and the church grew with new converts to the Christian faith.

Several chapters later in Acts 6, the early church was confronted with racism that affected the poor. The Greek widows were excluded from the daily distribution of food. The church corrected the problem by diversifying its leadership, appointing men from among the disenfranchised group of Greeks to serve in positions of power. A new group of deacons was empowered to redistribute the resources of the church more equitably, ensuring that the Greek widows were included in the daily distribution of food. The needs of the poor were again being met, as the church adhered to the spirit of the tithe.

Reconsider How You Tithe

In the story of Lazarus, the rich man either forgot or more likely forsook the teachings found in the law and the prophets. Like the shepherds of Israel in Ezekiel 34 and the scribes in Luke 20, the rich man chose to enhance his own lifestyle to the neglect of the poor. He chose not to see the needs of his neighbor, hiding behind the gate he had built to secure himself from the problems of his neighbors. His decision was short-sighted.

Daily, Jesus gives us opportunities to tear down the metaphorical gates that separate us from the poor. We pass by people entrapped by poverty every day. Moses said, "The poor you will always have with you; therefore, open your hand to the poor" (Deuteronomy 15:11). We need to open our eyes to see the poor as people to be loved and not as problems to be solved. As we invite the poor to be our friends and neighbors, we tear down Satan's strongholds. The barriers between rich and poor give way to the love of Jesus expressed through his church.

The Bible encourages us to give out of the generosity that we have received from the Lord. Instead of fearing the future, and hoarding resources to secure a certain quality of life for ourselves, we should give generously to others, trusting that God will provide for us during our time of need. We are to give, not begrudgingly, but with glad and generous hearts in celebration of the grace we have received.

The way we apportion our money says a lot about the things we love. Our giving is a good barometer of Christ's command to love our neighbors. The rich man segregated himself from the poor and spent his resources lavishly upon himself. His behaviors betrayed the condition of his heart. Absent of faith that leads to love, he was condemned to hell. We would be well advised to sit down with our church leaders and examine the priorities defined by our church budgets. Is there a significant apportionment for mission work and relief of the poor, or do our church budgets betray our tendency to support ministries that serve ourselves?

I am proud to be part of a church that takes the spirit of the tithe to heart. Weekly, we share a meal together during our church gatherings, giving thanks to God for his provision. Our meals are a reflection of the spirit of the tithe, celebrating the grace and generosity God has shown to our community. Our church meetings include time for discussing how to redistribute financial gifts to those in need. We prioritize caring for the poor over church programs and events. Those priorities are reflected in our church budget. Ninety percent of our giving supports missionaries and local ministry efforts to help those in poverty.

Having the ability to redistribute resources to those in need is a rich and rewarding part of our faith that is finding expression through our tithe. My hope is that everyone who reads this book would take the time to discuss with their church leaders how to use their tithe as an instrument of God's love, giving generously to those in need. Use the questions below to guide your discussion on giving to the poor. What changes are you willing to make to reflect God's commandment to give to the poor in their time of need?

Questions for Reflection

1. Intentionally or unintentionally, how do you separate yourself from people in poverty?
2. Loving our neighbors often entails sacrificial giving. How are you giving to those in need?
3. Request a copy of your church's budget. What percentage of the budget is allocated to support ministries for the congregation, and what percentage is allocated to caring for the poor?
4. Does your church's budget reflect God's generosity to the poor? What changes can you make to reflect God's priorities?

CHAPTER 8

LOVE YOUR NEIGHBOR

"Is not this the kind of fasting I have chosen: to loose the chains of injustice and untie the cords of the yoke, to set the oppressed free and break every yoke? Is it not to share your food with the hungry and to provide the poor wanderer with shelter— when you see the naked, to clothe them, and not to turn away from your own flesh and blood?"
Isaiah 58:6-7

When I was in seminary, I lived with a couple of classmates in a hundred-year-old house in downtown Lexington, KY. We were a part of a small group of people from Asbury Theological Seminary who were starting a church among the homeless. I went home to Memphis for a couple of weeks during the first winter break that we lived in the house. While I was gone, one of my roommates invited John, a homeless friend, to live with him while I was gone.

John, thankful to be off the snowy streets of Lexington, cranked up the heat in our house and was enjoying a Caribbean winter. We received a $700 utility bill soon after I returned from Christmas vacation. I was upset. The bill was way beyond what we had budgeted. I lowered the thermostat to 55 degrees and wouldn't let my roommates turn the thermostat any higher until we figured out how to pay for our bill. The next month was worse. Our utility bill ballooned to $1300. I panicked. Our house was a sieve. Even after turning down the thermostat, warm air was escaping through the windows and under the doors. Our landlord was unresponsive to our request for help. He swore up and down that the previous tenants had never complained about the heat. He said we must be doing something wrong.

I humbled myself and wrote to my home church for help. I asked them to pay off our utility bill. I didn't know what else to do. They were kind and honored my request, but my roommates and I still had no long-term solution to our problem. Our house was so cold at night that I could see my own breath. I buried myself in a sleeping bag that I had purchased for a camping trip to Colorado. It was a lifesaver.

We finally got around to checking the attic to see if it was properly insulated. I discovered that the previous tenants had re-routed the heating vents to a makeshift closet in the attic where they were growing hallucinogenic mushrooms. No wonder they never complained to the landlord about their heat!

Our house sat between the University of Kentucky campus to the north and the YMCA to the south, where men took their first steps out of homelessness into efficiency apartments. The drug culture was strong on our street. Hallucinogenic mushrooms were complemented with paint huffing, a cheap alternative for getting high. In many ways, it was the perfect location for a ministry house. We were surrounded by University of Kentucky students and low-income urbanites. Common Grounds, a local coffee shop and our favorite hangout, was a couple blocks away. It was another easy walk in the opposite direction to the Bangkok House, which served the best pad Thai in the city. Other than a little heat in the winter, what more could we want?

Billy and Geoff were my roommates and fellow seminarians. Thoughtful and kind, Geoff had a quiet charisma. His Australian accent was developing a Southern drawl, much to his dismay. He was a model of Christian service, having developed humility from years of rooting for the lowly Magpies, his favorite Aussie football team. Geoff provided consistent theological reflection in our home, helping us to maintain a meaningful connection between spiritual devotion and social action.

Billy was one of the smartest people I knew. A weightlifter with a philosophy degree, he was gruff and merciful and spoke with the intensity of Al Sharpton. His furrowed brow and muscular physique hid a tender and generous heart. Billy had developed meaningful relationships with much of the homeless population in Downtown Lexington. The members of our fledgling church were developing relationships with the poor that he had initiated.

On occasion, Billy would bring his friends from the street to stay with us for a while. I can remember the first time I met Scott. He was shirtless and very hairy. His entire wardrobe consisted of a pair of jeans and an unbuttoned jean jacket, which offered little protection against the cold Kentucky winter. He also wore a red bandanna tied around his head.

The morning after Scott's first-night stay with us, I climbed out of my thermal sleeping bag (it was still freezing cold in our house) and went to the bathroom to warm up with a hot shower. When I opened the door to the bathroom, all the toilet paper had been unrolled. It was piled three feet high in the trash can next to the toilet. When I pulled back the curtain to get into the shower, all our silverware was in the bathtub. I decided to skip the shower and went to the kitchen to fix a cup of coffee. All our appliances had been re-arranged. The coffee pot was sitting on top of the coffee maker. I stared at it for several minutes, wondering why anyone would think it was better arranged that way.

Scott made his way into the kitchen as the coffee brewed and the bacon sizzled. We settled down to eat our breakfast with a couple of plastic spoons I found in the pantry. It was the first and last time I tried to eat bacon with a plastic spoon. As we ate, Scott and I got to know one another.

Scott wasn't shy. A flood of information poured forth as we talked together. Scott said he was a former NHL hockey player who played for the Minnesota North Stars before they relocated to Dallas. He had a lot of money in the bank, but he couldn't get to it because "the man" wouldn't give it to him. If he could only get his money back, he wouldn't be homeless anymore.

I didn't know what kind of mental illness Scott had, but I felt certain that "illusions of grandeur" must be part of the diagnosis. I finished breakfast and got in my car for the twenty-minute commute to the seminary. I left frustrated that my home had been turned upside down by Scott, and I was a little anxious about what he would do next. In my mind, there wasn't much hope for someone like Scott, and I didn't feel prepared to live with a stranger suffering from a serious mental illness. I confronted Billy about it later, asking how long Scott was going to be staying with us.

"A couple of days," Billy said. "Until I can help him get access to the money he has in the bank."

"What? Are you serious? You mean the story he told me was true?"

We were never able to confirm that Scott played in the NHL, but he did have a legitimate mental illness for which he received a regular disability check. Over $10,000 had built up in Scott's account, but the bank wouldn't release the money to him until someone signed off as his caretaker. Over the course of the next several days, Billy completed the paperwork to become Scott's legal guardian. Billy helped Scott access his money and secured a place for him to stay at the YMCA down the street from us. He also helped Scott get the medical attention he needed for his illness. Over time, Scott renewed relationships with his family and became a meaningful contributor to our faith community.

The Greatest Commandment

In many ways, John and Scott were experiencing the bondage of Satan's strongholds when we met them. Both struggled with mental illness and broken relationships. Billy took the initiative to love them as our neighbors. He entered into their world and encouraged Geoff and me to do the same.

By using the network of relationships that were available to him, Billy was able to help Scott break the downward cycle of poverty he was in. Billy modeled for me how to love my neighbor as myself. Love is the central value of God's kingdom. When we love others with the love of Christ, Satan's hold on the world diminishes. The gates of Hell receive a battering, and those within its grasp receive a tangible expression of God's grace.

When Jesus was asked by a religious leader, "What is the most important commandment in the Bible?" he gave a direct answer, "You shall love the Lord your God with all your heart and with all your soul and with all your strength and with all your mind, and your neighbor as yourself." (Luke 10:27). Jesus gives a clear directive for how to flourish in life and ministry: to love. The religious leader wasn't satisfied. The Bible says, "He wanted to justify himself," so he asked another question: "So, who is my neighbor?" The man's response reveals a very important lesson about our human nature: We desire to be in control. Like Adam and Eve in the garden, we want to determine for ourselves what is right and wrong. We don't like to be told what to do. We want to make the determination for ourselves. We want to decide who to love.

Jesus clarifies what he meant by loving our neighbor by telling the story of the Good Samaritan in Luke 10:30-37. You probably know the story already. It is one of the most well-known stories in the Bible. After all, if you are looking for a shortcut to understanding the Bible, why not jump to the spot where Jesus tells us what is most important?

In the story, a priest and a Levite travel down a dangerous road from Jerusalem to Jericho. The road was frequented by thieves who targeted individuals as they passed from one urban center to the other through the sparsely populated Judean wilderness. The priest sees a man lying on the side of the road. He has been beaten, bloodied, and left for dead. He passes the stranger without stopping to help. Was he afraid? The text doesn't say, but probably so. Maybe he thought the stranger was setting a trap, faking his injuries and preparing to attack anyone who was foolish enough to stop. We can't be certain of what motivated the priest to keep moving, but we can take an educated guess of what prevented him from stopping: a lack of compassion and an unwillingness to enter into the suffering of the stranger. The Levite follows in the footsteps of the priest who went before him. Ignoring the plight of the downtrodden man, he continues on his journey without stopping to help.

In contrast to the priest and the Levite, a Samaritan man sees the suffering of the stranger and stops to help. He bandages the man's wounds and carries him to a local hotel where he pays for his housing and medical care. Despite the cultural and religious differences that separated the Samaritan man and the man who was injured, the Samaritan demonstrated compassion. He loved his neighbor.

Like the priest and the Levite in the story of the good Samaritan, I wasn't prepared to engage with Scott in his plight. My heart was not sufficiently filled with God's mercy. Cynicism and self-interest squelched my compassion. When I looked at Scott, I saw a mentally ill homeless man. He was a stranger to me, and to some degree, he was a threat to the comfortable way of life I had grown accustomed to. His presence in my home meant that I would not be able to decompress after a long day of work. I felt threatened and thus emotionally guarded.

When Billy looked at Scott, he saw a neighbor in need of help. His heart was moved by compassion. He listened to Scott. Billy trusted him, took him at his word, and helped Scott explore potential solutions to his problems. He gave Scott the space he needed to decompress from the stress of homelessness, rather than hoarding the peace of our home to himself. Billy loaned Scott legitimacy at the bank and provided him with connectivity to medical and legal resources. When Scott was ready to repair the bridges he had burned with his family, Billy advocated on Scott's behalf. Billy loved his neighbor.

Restoring the Foundations of Society

The prophet Isaiah had a name for people like Billy: "a restorer of the breach." The title is an honor Isaiah bestowed upon people who worshiped God by extending hospitality to the marginalized. Isaiah said, "If you spend yourselves on behalf of the hungry and satisfy the needs of the oppressed" (Isaiah 58:10), then "Your people will rebuild the ancient ruins and will raise up the age-old foundations; you will be called Repairer of Broken Walls, Restorer of Streets with Dwellings" (Isaiah 58:12). Isaiah is saying that when we build relationships with the poor that are grounded in love and personal sacrifice, we begin the process of healing our civilization.

In Isaiah 58, God tells the prophet to rebuke the community of faith for their self-centered worship. On the surface, everything looked fine. The people of Israel sought God daily, delighted in knowing his ways, asked God for righteous judgments, and delighted in drawing near to God while fasting and humbling themselves. Translating those practices into contemporary Christian culture, we would say they had daily devotionals, attended church services, met in Bible studies, asked God to intervene in their lives, praised God in times of worship, and fasted to grow in spiritual discipline.

The problem according to Isaiah is that these spiritual practices did not translate into love for God and neighbor. While engaged in religious practices, business owners exploited their workers for their own private gain. The community was filled with strife and violence. Love, joy, and peace—signs of the Spirit of God at work—were missing.

God told the people of Israel that true worship was practiced by extending hospitality to those who were oppressed. Sharing a meal with someone who is hungry, bringing the homeless into your house, and clothing the naked are ways to worship God. God is not describing acts of charity done from afar. He is not talking about giving your excess clothes to Goodwill or passing out a meal at the local soup kitchen. He is talking about developing personal relationships with the poor by opening your home to people who are different than you. Love is the central act of worshiping God, and love is personal.

In the past decade, academics like Robert Putman have raised awareness about the importance of relationships to economic health. He describes *social capital* as the connectivity of relationships that opens economic opportunities and enhances community life. In his book, *Our Kids*, Dr. Putnam tells the story of Ned, one of his high school classmates, who grew up in poverty. The pastor of Ned's church helped Ned to apply for financial aid to college, which opened a new opportunity that might not have been available to him otherwise. The relationship between Ned and his pastor was a form of social capital. Dr. Putnam argues that since the 1950s social capital has decreased in America, we have isolated ourselves by social class, which limits opportunities for economic advancement.

Isaiah makes the case that worshiping God necessitates extending love and hospitality to those who are poor. Increasingly, the poor and the wealthy are living in isolation from one another. We don't know each other's strengths and vulnerabilities, and our community is poorer for it. Like the walls of an ancient city, relationships built on trust that cross class lines actually protect us from danger by providing connections to people who can help us in times of trouble.

When Billy met Scott, Scott's social capital had been spent. Scott didn't have the relationships he needed to access the basic necessities of life. The lack of relationships left Scott vulnerable. Billy enhanced Scott's social capital, connecting him to the institutions and individuals who could help him. In turn, Scott enriched our lives by putting a human face on homelessness. Scott helped us to understand the trauma and isolation that contributes to poverty.

The church, men and women of faith who have crucified their self-interests to follow Christ, who have received God's grace, who possess the Spirit of God, have been empowered to reverse the oppression and isolation that perpetuates poverty. When we heed Isaiah's call to worship God by extending hospitality to the poor, we begin the process of restoring our society. By sharing our lives with the poor, we extend God's grace in the world and open opportunities for us to thrive together.

I encourage you to look for practical ways to build meaningful relationships with the poor and then help them to connect to people in your circle of influence. If you are struggling to think of practical ways to love the poor, try following Billy's example. Billy built relationships with men in our community by hanging out at coffee shops where the homeless gathered to get out of the cold. He bought them coffee and asked them questions about their lives. He would go back to the same places several times a month to establish relationships with the regulars. As he got to know people better, he started to introduce them to other people he knew, like Geoff and me. By helping the poor to expand their social network, new opportunities for social advancement arise.

If you desire to be a restorer of the breach, you must be intentional in building relationships with the poor. Our culture is moving in the opposite direction, teaching us to isolate and protect ourselves from the problems of poverty. You can prepare yourself to love the poor through prayer, asking God to give you opportunities to meet people who are different than you.

Be mindful that the poor are often in crisis. Like the good Samaritan who went out of his way to help the man who had been beaten on the side of the road, relationships with the poor can't be scheduled. You will need to maintain a level of flexibility to respond to the needs of the poor.

I've built many relationships with the poor simply by responding to requests for help. I have helped people find jobs by introducing them to friends of mine who work in the construction business. I have helped men who can't read fill out job applications and apply for identification cards, birth certificates, and social security cards. I've accompanied men to their medical appointments and assisted people to apply for disability coverage. But almost none of these activities were initially scheduled. I had to adjust my priorities to make room for the poor.

These opportunities for service have been mutually beneficial. Spending time helping others has helped me to learn about the brokenness of our social systems. I now understand the difficulties people face as they try to break out of poverty.

The important thing to remember as you develop new friendships with the poor is to keep mutual love at the center of your relationships. It is easy to look at the poor as people to be fixed. God desires more than that. By truly loving one another, sharing our lives together, and learning from one another, we rebuild the very fabric of our society. God breaks the social injustices we create out of our selfish ambitions by teaching us to love one another.

Questions for Reflection

1. How does Isaiah 58:1-12 expand your understanding of worship?
2. What are a few practical steps you would be willing to take to build friendships with the poor?
3. How can you use your network of relationships to help people out of poverty?

CHAPTER 9

CULTIVATE A SPIRIT OF GENEROSITY

"Give to everyone who begs from you."
Luke 6:30

I hate this verse. I wish it wasn't in the Bible. At the very least, I wish Jesus had qualified his command to make it more palatable. When confronted with giving money to someone in need, my mind races. What if I give money to him and he uses it for alcohol or drugs? What if my gift unintentionally builds dependency instead of empowering him to stand on his own? Shouldn't I be willing to do more than give a handout? Should I make a greater commitment of time to build a friendship?

After reading Luke 6:30 during a morning devotional, I struggled to reconcile the practical lessons I'd learned about giving in the inner city with the seemingly impractical advice of Jesus. I disagreed with Jesus' "advice" to give to anyone who begged from me. In my mind, alms-giving was an outdated model of philanthropy that robbed the poor of their dignity. Bob Lupton's *Toxic Charity* and Brian Fickert's *When Helping Hurts* make compelling cases for limiting unidirectional giving to relief efforts in times of emergency. They argue that some forms of charity can lead to dependency and limit the development of human potential. A more nuanced approach focusing on human development and community efforts to address systemic causes of poverty is needed.

Jesus' words "give to anyone who begs of you" chaffed me. I didn't know how to reconcile Jesus' teaching with Bob and Brian's wisdom on giving, developed through their years of extensive research and faithful ministry. To relieve the burden I felt, I decided to conduct a social experiment. I never carry cash with me, but I prepared myself to obey Jesus' teaching without trying to rationalize it. I withdrew $100 from the bank and kept small denominations of $10s, $5s, and $1s in my billfold. Whenever someone asked me for money, I would give it to them, without presumption or qualification. I committed to journaling my experiences to glean additional truth through further reflection. A boxing match was ensuing in my imagination with Bob and Brian in one corner and Jesus in the other. The next couple of weeks would determine the winner.

The next Saturday, I was sitting in my house reading a magazine. The blinds were open, my children were playing outside with the neighbors, and I was enjoying a few minutes of quiet solitude. Through the window, I saw Philip, a ten-year-old boy, riding his bike through my yard. He pulled right up to my door and started banging on it. I was angry. I didn't want to be disturbed, and I was upset that Philip had driven his bike through my front lawn.

"What do you want, Philip?" I asked.

"Give me some water."

"No. I'm not giving you any water, Philip. You live one block down the street. Look, I can see your grandma right there. Go home and get yourself a glass of water."

Philip had disturbed my peace, and I was angry. I closed the door, and Philip rode off. As soon as he was gone, Luke 6:30 popped into my mind: "Give to everyone who begs from you." I had prepared myself to give money to a beggar. I wasn't prepared to give a glass of water to my neighbor. *Is God testing me?* I thought to myself. Another Bible verse ran through my mind. "Whoever gives one of these little ones even a cup of cold water because he is a disciple, truly, I say to you, he will by no means lose his reward" (Matthew 10:42).

I missed an opportunity to be generous to my young neighbor. I was more concerned with my grass and the interruption of my day than I was with fulfilling Philip's request. For the moment, I had lost a reward, a blessing God was offering through the request of a child. I missed an opportunity to sit on the front porch with Philip, enjoying a cold drink on a warm day in Memphis. I missed an opportunity for the conversation that would ensue and the relationship that would be built through a simple act of kindness. At least now I was prepared. I wouldn't miss the next chance to be generous.

On Wednesday, I pulled my truck into my driveway, parked and began unloading my lawnmower. It had been at the small engine shop getting a tune-up. The engine shop was only open from 9 am to 4 pm, Monday through Friday, so my lunch break was the only opportunity I had to retrieve my mower. It took longer than expected to pay my bill and load the mower into my truck. I felt pressed for time. I needed to get back to the office. As I unloaded the lawnmower, another young neighbor named Kobe approached me.

"Nathan, let me cut your lawn," Kobe said.

"You know I am a little particular about how my lawn is cut, Kobe. I kind of like cutting it myself. By the way, why aren't you in school today?"

"What do you mean?"

"I mean it is twelve o'clock on a school day. Why aren't you in school?"

"Cause my teacher lied on me."

"What did she say?"

"She said I threw a book at her. She got me suspended."

"Did you throw a book at her?"

"Yeah, but I shouldn't have gotten suspended for it."

I was opening the gate to my backyard as we talked. "I don't think I want you to cut my yard today, Kobe."

Kobe walked back across the street to his house, and I finished putting the lawnmower away when Luke 6:30 ran through my mind again. "Give to everyone who begs from you." Kobe asked for a small job, not a handout. I was still running my experiment and had yet to give away any of the money in my wallet. I was really bad at this. I changed my mind and decided to give Kobe the job after all. I walked across the street and knocked on the door to his house. An older man whom I didn't recognize answered the door. I could see Kobe in the background playing video games.

"Can I help you?"

"Yes, you can. Kobe asked if he could cut my grass. The job is worth about $30. Would you be willing to cut my yard for me and have Kobe help you with it? I'll pay you, and you can give Kobe whatever you think is fair for his contribution to the work."

"Sure. We would be happy to do it."

Again, Kobe had caught me off guard. I was looking to give money away to a beggar. I wasn't prepared to give a job to my neighbor. My thinking was still too rigid. My experiment wasn't developing the way I had hoped.

A couple of days passed, and Saturday rolled around again. I had received a lumber delivery for a shed I was building in my backyard. The lumber was piled neatly at the end of the driveway. As I was carrying the lumber to the backyard, Ray walked up. Ray was the man I had met a couple of days before at Kobe's house. He had done an excellent job of cutting my lawn while Kobe ran the trimmer. I learned that Ray and Renisha, Kobe's mom, were dating. Ray asked if he could help me build my shed. I knew that I still had $70 left in my "Give to Whomever Asks of You" experiment, but I didn't feel like it was enough money to pay for the labor it would require to build the shed. So I told Ray, "No thanks. I don't think I have enough money to pay you for the work."

"I don't want your money, Nathan. I want to be a good neighbor and help you build your shed."

Man, am I an idiot, I thought to myself.

It turned out that Ray was an accomplished carpenter and quite handy with a nail gun. We had the shed framed and decked before the day was over. After work, we sat together and enjoyed a glass of iced tea. Easter was around the corner, and Ray began to ask me questions about the upcoming holiday.

"Does your family do an Easter egg hunt?" Ray asked.

"Sometimes," I said. "But our favorite Easter tradition is to celebrate the Passover meal with our church. Have you heard of Passover before?"

"No, what is it?"

I explained the rich tradition of the Jewish Passover, of how God delivered the Israelites from their slavery in Egypt. I explained how Pharaoh refused to release the Israelites, so God sent plagues on Egypt for Pharaoh's disobedience. I told Ray about the last plague of death and how God saved his people by instructing them to spread the blood of a lamb on the doorposts of their homes. When the angel of death saw the blood of the lamb, he passed over the house, sparing the residents inside from God's wrath. I explained how the story foreshadowed the death of Jesus. Jesus was the lamb of God who came to take away the sins of the world (John 1:29). I explained that we celebrate Easter because it signifies Jesus' victory over sin and death. It stands as a reminder that when we receive Jesus as our covering, we are spared from the eternal consequences of our sin. We will experience a bodily resurrection like Jesus and will live with him forever.

Ray had gone to church off and on for most of his life but had never heard anyone explain the meaning of Easter to him.

After I finished telling the story, Ray looked at me and asked, "Can I come to church with you?" Ray wasn't looking for a handout. He wasn't even asking for a job. He was "begging" for Christian fellowship.

How to Soften a Hardened Heart

God reveals the meaning of scripture as we put his words into practice. Reading the Bible helped me to understand that as a follower of Jesus, God expected me to be generous. As I put the scripture into practice, I came to understand the depth of my sin and the need for God's grace. In time, the condition of my heart began to change. I actually became more generous.

After my experiment was over, I realized that I was asking the wrong questions. I had created a false dichotomy in my mind by pitting Bob and Brian against Jesus. The point of Jesus' teaching was to be generous to everyone in their time of need. Sometimes, people are in a crisis and in need of a handout. Other times, they need a job or companionship.

By trying to put Luke 6:20 into practice, God showed me that my heart was hard. I was stingy and narrow-minded. I was emotionally withdrawn from my neighbors and hardened to the movement of the Holy Spirit. I needed a new heart to extend God's grace to others and new eyes to see the spiritual dynamics that were at work all around me. My natural inclination when asked for anything was to say no. I was selfish. I wanted to protect my time and my possessions. Even after preparing myself to be generous, it took time for me to develop a spirit of generosity. God's word revealed my sinfulness and the need for his grace.

There is a danger in studying God's word without putting it into action. We can submerge ourselves in sermons and Bible studies and wrongly believe that we are growing in devotion to God. My heart had been hardened through years of studying God's word but failing to put it into action. The book of James warns us against such hypocrisy. "But be doers of the word, and not hearers only, deceiving yourselves. For if anyone is a hearer of the word and not a doer, he is like a man who looks intently at his natural face in a mirror. For he looks at himself and goes away and at once forgets what he was like. But the one who looks into the perfect law, the law of liberty, and perseveres, being no hearer who forgets but a doer who acts, he will be blessed in his doing" (James 1:22-25). After committing to obey the word of God, in addition to meditating on it, I began to grow in generosity toward my neighbors.

I also learned that I was a beggar in need of God's grace. God used the command, "Give to everyone who begs of you," to show me that I was impoverished by a lack of generosity in my life. By receiving God's grace with a humble heart, I would be better prepared to extend his grace to others.

The Greek word for *grace* is *charisma*. The word for spiritual gifts is *charismata*. God's grace (charisma) flows through us and is expressed as his spiritual gifts (charismata) in the world. The church is a conduit of God's grace. Like a light that shines on a prism, God's grace is refracted through the church and is expressed in the world as a diversity of gifts such as mercy, service, and generosity (Romans 12:3-8).

Without God's grace actively moving through me, the stinginess of my flesh was expressed in my relationships with others. When mindful of God's word, the Holy Spirit brought conviction and correction to my actions. God's generosity was able to flow through me to my neighbors.

Learning Scripture through Obedience

There are some passages of scripture that only will open the rich bounty of God's wisdom through active obedience. Jesus ends the Sermon on the Mount with the story of the wise and foolish builders. The wise man built his house on a rock. When the storms of life hit his house, it remained standing because the foundation was solid. The foolish man built his house on sand. When the storms came and the winds blew, his house collapsed.

When I ask people what this story is about, they generally say that if Jesus is the foundation of our lives, we will stand firm against life's trials. It is a nice sentiment but not exactly the point of Jesus' story. Jesus tells us exactly what the story means in Matthew 7:24. "Everyone then who hears these words of mine and does them will be like a wise man who built his house on the rock." God's word is not just to be studied. It is meant to be acted upon.

I fear that many of us attend church services and Bible studies trying to acquire greater knowledge of God's word without ever acting upon his teachings. To hear God's word and to know its meaning but not act upon it is foolish and will lead to our destruction. Obedience to God's word is the bedrock that undergirds a wise and fruitful life.

The scribes in Herod's entourage are examples of foolish men who knew about the Messiah from their study of the prophets (Matthew 2:1-12) but refused to act in submission to their teaching. They didn't look for Jesus to worship him like the wise men from the east. Using the scribe's knowledge of Jesus' birthplace, Herod issued an edict to slaughter the male children of Bethlehem, hoping to maintain his power by killing the Messiah before he was able to establish his kingdom. The scribes' knowledge of the Messiah through the Old Testament scriptures led to death and destruction. Only when we align our lives in obedience to Jesus' teachings will God be honored and our communities blessed through God's word.

Before my experiment in obedience, I felt stuck as I pondered the meaning of "give to everyone who begs of you." After trying to obey the command, I was more aware of my sinfulness and my need for God's grace. I had experienced the power of the Holy Spirit to convict and correct me. As I sat and talked with Ray, I discovered the joy that generosity brings to a community. Through trial and error, I learned the value of generosity.

Since my social experiment, I have felt greater freedom to be generous with my time, my money, and my relationships. I'm not as worried about misinterpreting scripture. If I screw up, I know God will gracefully bring correction, pointing me back in the direction he wants me to go. As I obey God through the grace he gives to me, He is glorified, and my experience of community is enriched. As a beggar before Jesus, I experience the kindness of his mercy and am grateful for his lessons on generosity and obedience.

I encourage you to repeat my experiment and journal what you learn. Read and meditate on Luke 6:17-36. Record what you think the passage of scripture is about. Withdraw $100 in small bills from your bank account and be prepared to give the money away to anyone who asks of you (Luke 6:30). Be patient and prepared to respond with generosity. Again, record the giving events in your journal. Pay special attention to the condition of your heart before, during, and after the experiment. Do you feel anxious and afraid, grateful or resentful? Do you experience joy in giving to others? How do your feelings change as the experiment progresses? Each time you give to others, reflect on Luke 6:17-36 again. Are there aspects of the scripture that have a deeper or more nuanced meaning for you now?

This type of experiment can be performed with any of Jesus' commands. When we study the scriptures, we should do so with the intention of putting what we read into practice. God will teach us as much if not more from our application of the scriptures as we learn from our times of reading and reflection. God changes the affections of our hearts as we faithfully obey his commands.

Questions for Reflection

1. What are some common barriers that prevent people from being generous with others?
2. What steps of obedience do you want to take to grow in generosity?

CHAPTER 10

FORGIVENESS: THE POWER OF THE GOSPEL

"For if you forgive other people when they sin against you, your heavenly Father will also forgive you. But if you do not forgive others their sins, your Father will not forgive your sins."
Matthew 16:14-15

About two years ago, my neighbor Carol and her family experienced trauma. Carol's son, Diego, was tragically shot and killed. Unfortunately, her experience is common in communities like ours, but Carol possesses an uncommon grace that flows from her deep devotion to Jesus Christ. Her ability to forgive her son's assailant is a testament to the grace of God in her. Throughout my experience in urban ministry, I have found that forgiveness is one of the most powerful virtues of the Christian faith. It can provide the greatest good and bring the greatest healing to the wounds we accumulate, but giving and receiving forgiveness is seldom practiced.

Ian was an intern in our residency program at the time of Diego's death. He and his wife Tara lived across the street from Carol, just down the street from our family. I asked Ian to recount the night of Diego's death. Here is Ian's story in his own words:

I got home late from the inpatient service at Baptist Hospital. When I pulled into my driveway, I thought it was odd that my neighbor didn't pop his head out and say hello like he always did. I was glad to make it to the door without any interruptions that night. I was exhausted.

Tara had dinner ready when I got home. After we started eating, there was a loud knock at the door. I didn't want to be disturbed. I wanted to eat and go to sleep. When the knock came again, I decided I needed to open the door. It was Montez. He usually didn't come over that late at night. He had no expression on his face. I asked, "Montez, what's wrong?" He stood there for a long time without saying anything. I asked again, "Montez, what's going on? What do you need?" All he could say was, "My brother's dead." Both of us were in shock. I kept thinking, *which one of your brothers is dead?* But the only word that came out of my mouth was, "What?"

We asked him to come inside. Tara started putting the pieces together. It was probably Diego who died, but Montez couldn't talk about it. He was sobbing, grieving over the loss of his brother. No one in Montez's family was at home that night. A friend was waiting for him on his porch when Montez arrived at the house. "Your brother was shot. He's dead," his friend had said.

That's when Montez came to us for help. He thought his mom might be down the street at their church, so we took him there. When we got to the church, police cars were blocking the intersection. The parking lot of the church was packed. There were people everywhere. Neighbors, police, church members, gang members, small children, and even the media were there. People were standing around staring at the police, not knowing what to do. We got out and started searching the crowd for Carol. There were a bunch of police cars across the street from the church with blue lights flashing. We saw a body lying in the parking lot surrounded by police tape.

We wandered through the crowd until we found Mary, the pastor's wife. She pointed us to Carol, and we brought Montez to her. Carol was wailing. She could barely stand up. Somebody brought a chair from the church and made her sit down. She kept screaming, "My baby, my baby." Montez went over and stood next to her. He still had a glazed look on his face. There were tons of people screaming and crying. Others from the crowd were consoling each other saying, "At least Diego is in heaven now. At least he is in heaven with Jesus."

I found pastor Shun and asked him why people kept saying that about Diego. He had a reputation for running from the Lord. Carol had been praying for her son for years, praying that he would come to know Jesus as his savior. Pastor Shun said, "Diego came to the church service last night and told everybody he was leaving the gang. He wanted to start his life over. He made a decision to follow Christ." Diego's salvation was a glimmer of light in the midst of great darkness.

The next day, Tara went to check on Ms. Carol. Carol said she forgave the person for shooting Diego. She said, "I don't even know who it is, but I already forgave 'em. It's not us. It's the sin in us that caused all this."

The next night, there was a candlelight vigil in front of Carol's house. The news crews came out again. There were a bunch of people there from Carol's church, her extended family, and other people from the neighborhood. People were crouching around, lighting candles after it got dark.

There was a lady there who spoke. Her son had also been killed by gun violence. She talked about putting aside the desire to retaliate. She said that vengeance wasn't the answer. Then Pastor Shun talked about sin, forgiveness, and ending the cycle of violence in our neighborhood. It was very powerful.

After Ian recounted the series of events surrounding Diego's death, I asked Carol how she found the strength to forgive the person who had killed her son. She said, "We have to forgive.

God forgives us of our sin so we can forgive other people of their sins." She also said, "The person who shot my baby doesn't need my hatred. She needs my love. She needs God's love. She needs forgiveness."

Finding the Strength to Forgive

Forgiveness is the power of the gospel. It restores broken relationships and breaks the cycle of violence that plagues impoverished communities. Forgiveness helps those who have been traumatized to heal from anger and bitterness. Carol was able to forgive the person who shot her son because she had experienced God's forgiveness herself. Jesus forgives us of our sins so we will have the grace to forgive others.

Jesus told his disciples a parable about an unforgiving servant to teach them the importance of forgiveness:

> Peter came up and said to him, "Lord, how often will my brother sin against me, and I forgive him? As many as seven times?" Jesus said to him, "I do not say to you seven times, but seventy-seven times.
>
> "Therefore the kingdom of heaven may be compared to a king who wished to settle accounts with his servants. When he began to settle, one was brought to him who owed him ten thousand talents. And since he could not pay, his master ordered him to be sold, with his wife and children and all that he had, and payment to be made.
>
> "So the servant fell on his knees, imploring him, 'Have patience with me, and I will pay you everything.' And out of pity for him, the master of that servant released him and forgave him the debt.

> "But when that same servant went out, he found one of his fellow servants who owed him a hundred denarii, and seizing him, he began to choke him, saying, 'Pay what you owe.' So his fellow servant fell down and pleaded with him, 'Have patience with me, and I will pay you.' He refused and went and put him in prison until he should pay the debt.
>
> "When his fellow servants saw what had taken place, they were greatly distressed, and they went and reported to their master all that had taken place. Then his master summoned him and said to him, 'You wicked servant! I forgave you all that debt because you pleaded with me. And should not you have had mercy on your fellow servant, as I had mercy on you?' And in anger, his master delivered him to the jailers until he should pay all his debt.
>
> "So also my heavenly Father will do to every one of you if you do not forgive your brother from your heart" (Matthew 18:21-35).

One talent was the equivalent of fifteen years of salary for a day laborer. Since the servant owed 10,000 talents, it would have taken him 150,000 years to repay his debt to the king—an impossible task. To put the man's debt into today's terms, the servant owed the king $4.5 billion dollars.

The servant's only hope for debt relief was to seek the king's forgiveness. Only the king had the power to release the debt for such a large sum of money. But that's not what the servant did. He asked for more time to repay the debt. The man was clearly a fool. He didn't understand the extent of his financial condition. He didn't understand his own limitations that kept him from honoring his obligation to the king, nor did he grasp the graceful nature of the king he served. The king took pity on the fool. The king's forgiveness was rooted in his own mercy, not in anything the servant said or did.

Instead of receiving the king's mercy with gratefulness, the servant foolishly tried to collect the debts that were owed to him. It is clear that the king's mercy did not inspire the servant to be merciful to others. His fellow servant owed him 1,000 denarii. A denarius was a day's wage. Again, converting the debt into today's wages, the man owed the servant about $120,000. That is no small sum of money until it is compared to the $4.5 billion the servant owed the king.

The servant's heart was filled with anger and aggression. He lashed out at his co-worker when he was not immediately able to repay the debt. The servant turned to the law, demanding that justice be served, holding his co-worker to account for his indebtedness.

Unforgiveness creates vicious cycles that cripple people and communities alike. Carol didn't want to perpetuate the cycle of retributive justice that often accompanies gang-related crime.

It was later discovered that Diego was shot by a girl who belonged to a gang. It was a case of mistaken identity. In the darkness of night, she thought Diego was someone else. She thought he belonged to a rival gang and was enacting a form of justice for a crime she believed had been perpetrated against her. When her identity became known, members of the gang Diego had belonged to wanted retribution. The girl was already in police custody, but several gang members decided they would take their anger out on the girl's sister who attended the middle school in our neighborhood.

Word got out to the police that the girl was going to be jumped after school. Both the middle school and the elementary school that shares a campus with it were put on lockdown. My children were in attendance at the elementary school that day. While nothing became of the incident, my family experienced the fear that accompanies retaliatory violence.

Unforgiveness complicates and compounds the problem of community violence. Some of the patients who came to our community health clinic had been the victims of gang violence. Many more had been victims of sexual assault and domestic abuse. Their trauma was compounded by anger, which often expressed itself in unintentional ways. Our patients would report lashing out at friends and family members who had no direct connection to their original trauma.

Forgiveness is needed for personal healing, for recovering from the traumas that we experience at the hands of others. Satan desires to keep us in the emotional bondage that is created when someone sins against us (2 Corinthians 2:10-11). Forgiveness comes from God. As told in the story of the unforgiving servant, we forgive others because God has forgiven us.

Forgiven to Love

Jesus paid for the sins of the world so that we would serve God with our new-found freedom. "He himself bore our sins in his body on the cross, so that, free from sins, we might live for righteousness; by his wounds you have been healed" (1 Peter 2:24). Jesus forgave us, not because we asked for it or because we deserved it, but because he loved us. "In this is love, not that we loved God but that he loved us and sent his Son to be the atoning sacrifice for our sins. Beloved, since God loved us so much, we also ought to love one another" (1 John 4:11-12). God's love empowers us to love and forgive others even when they don't deserve it. God is our source for forgiveness, not the presence or absence of our offender's repentance.

Forgiveness releases the bitterness that grows up in our hearts when we think about the sin that was committed against us. Satan wants to use that bitterness to entrap us and to keep us from experiencing the peace that flows from God's grace. Instead of meditating on the sinful action that was committed against us, we are freed from bitterness when we meditate on God's grace.

"Guard against turning back from the grace of God. Let no one become like a bitter plant that grows up and causes many troubles with its poison" (Hebrews 12:14-15). Bitterness that is not confronted will destroy the relationships we have with other people. To experience the freedom that God desires for us, we must confront the source of our bitterness through forgiveness.

The Greek word for *forgiveness* in the Bible is *synchoresi*, which means release. When we forgive someone, we release the indebtedness they owe to us. We release them into the hands of God. By doing so, we experience freedom from our captivity to anger, resentment, and bitterness. Forgiving others does not mean that people will not be punished for their crimes. When we forgive someone, we release them from our anger and vengeance. We give them over to God (Romans 12:19) and to the authorities whom he appoints (Romans 13:1-4).

Many men in our neighborhood suffer the consequences of unforgiveness in our society. Having served time in jail for criminal activity in their past, they face the threat of chronic unemployment. When background checks reveal they have a felony on their record, employers are unwilling to hire them. Many spend the rest of their lives paying for their mistakes. They are never released from their indebtedness.

Very few companies will even give an interview to someone who has a felony on their record. Felons are viewed as a liability, a potential threat to the company. Employers who are willing to hire ex-felons often have to overcome economic disincentives for doing so. Many insurance companies raise premiums on liability insurance for companies that hire felons. Our society is not equipped to forgive. We need the church to practice forgiveness by giving men an opportunity to start over, releasing them from the debts of their past.

As I have worked with men in our community to find jobs, many have given up hope. They have been rejected so many times because of background checks that they've stopped looking for employment. Last year, word got out that a large warehouse was temporarily disbanding its policy of performing background checks on new employees to meet demand for its products before Christmas. Men in the neighborhood quickly jumped on the opportunity for employment. Once the demand for its products had been met, the company re-instituted its background check policy. New applicants for those jobs weren't as forthcoming anymore.

Forgiveness is a key virtue in God's kingdom and is noticeably absent in the kingdoms of this world. It is more than a social construct between individuals. Forgiveness builds and expands God's kingdom. It may be the most tangible demonstration of God's grace that we can experience in this world. Forgiveness reveals God's very nature. It is the centerpiece of the most important moment in human history: the crucifixion and resurrection of Christ. It is also next to impossible to put into practice on our own. Forgiveness is foreign to our human nature and contrasts with our view of justice, but it is essential to God's kingdom.

When forgiveness is offered to sinful people, God's kingdom grows. When forgiveness is given to those who have hurt us, bitterness loses its grip on our hearts and we experience God's peace. When forgiveness is offered to ex-felons, new opportunities are created, and economic prosperity can flow to impoverished communities.

Carol showed our community how to forgive. She reminded me that God took the initiative to forgive us even when we were sinners. Through the grace we received from Christ, we can forgive others, releasing them from our anger and healing our bitterness. Nothing builds a Christian community like forgiveness. God's kingdom can't exist without it. That's why

Jesus used such striking language to compel his followers to practice forgiveness. "If you don't forgive your neighbor for the sin that he committed against you, then neither will you be forgiven by God" (Matthew 6:15).

If you are struggling to forgive someone who has hurt you, or if your community has experienced significant trauma, try writing out a prayer of lament and forgiveness. A lament is a passionate expression of the grief we feel. A lament validates the feelings of betrayal or abuse we have experienced. It can help us identify the source of our anger and bitterness, enabling us to release those who have offended us to God. When partnered with forgiveness, a lament can be a powerful source of healing in our lives.

A prayer of lament contains five parts: (1) calling out to God, (2) describing your complaint, (3) requesting help, (4) expressing faith in God, (5) and vowing to praise God. Here is a prayer of lament and forgiveness that I wrote for our community after Carol's son was shot and killed in our neighborhood by a teenage girl. It is broken into the five categories that I described above. You can use it as a model for writing your own prayer of lament and forgiveness.

> Hear our cry, O God. Hear our cries for justice and mercy.
>
> Our neighborhood is devastated by violence. Children are killing children with weapons made by man. Our hearts are growing hard, and our love is growing cold. Anger and bitterness are taking root in our community.
>
> Break the cycle of violence we've created. Forgive us of our sins, so we can forgive each other.
>
> We trust in the power of your resurrection. We have faith that you will bring life from death.

> We praise you for your healing power, for sacrificing your Son so we don't have to sacrifice ours.

The questions below are provided to help you identify your need for forgiveness. One of the main ways Satan keeps us bound in spiritual strongholds is through unforgiveness. I want you to experience the peace and liberty that comes from being forgiven and forgiving others. Take time to answer the questions for reflection below. Ask God to show you if there is someone in your life you need to forgive. If a face or a name flashes in your mind as you pray, don't push the image away. Release that person to God. I encourage you to say his or her name out loud as you pray, "God I forgive ______."

Forgiveness is not a one-time act. It is a continual process of releasing those who cause us harm to God. It is God's responsibility to bring that person to a place of repentance or justice. Open your heart to the healing God can provide by forgiving those who have offended you.

Questions for Reflection

1. Are you experiencing anger or bitterness because someone has sinned against you?
2. Spend time reflecting on your own sin and brokenness. How have you sinned against God? Have you asked for and received His forgiveness?
3. After receiving God's forgiveness for your own sin, ask God if there is someone you need to forgive. Release them from your anger and into God's control.

CHAPTER 11

GO AND BEAR FRUIT

"You did not choose me, but I chose you and appointed you that you should go and bear fruit."
John 15:16

Over the years, I've had the opportunity to befriend some amazing people from our neighborhood who have persevered through difficult circumstances to become faithful disciples of Jesus. I first met Johnny Doe when he was a high school student and a recent immigrant to our country. Johnny survived a rough childhood to become an amazing man of God. He is now a worship leader for our church and works as a chaplain for Christ Community Health Services, a Christian clinic that serves our community. In many ways, Johnny's life reflects the principles described in this book. I asked Johnny to share in his own words how God saved him and set him apart for Christian service:

My life was hard. As a child, I experienced things that were unacceptable and unexplainable. I'm originally from Liberia, a country in West Africa. When I was seven years old, war broke out in my country. I was at my house with my family on a Sunday morning. We could hear gunshots and people screaming outside. The gunshots were getting closer to our house. As soon as we stepped outside to see what was going on,

I was separated from most of my family. I never saw my mom again. The whole street was full of people. Everybody was crying and running for their lives. I met a lady in the crowd who knew my grandmother. She grabbed my hand. She took me and my auntie to stay with her in Ghana for a while.

I was told that rebels had taken over Liberia. The fighting went on for a long time. So, my auntie and I moved around from place to place. We stayed with a lot of different people during this time. Some people took good care of me. Some people mistreated me because I wasn't their child. I had so much anger and frustration in my heart because everything was beyond my control and understanding. I wanted to know what had caused the war. Why was there so much hatred in us, as a people? My life felt empty. There was no hope. I believed the lies of the enemy. I used to think, this is the end of my life. You might as well get used to it, Johnny; nothing's going to change.

My auntie found out that her older brother had escaped to Ghana, so she sent me to stay at his house. My uncle was a hustler. I'm not exactly sure what he did for a living, but he was never at home. He would give me some money and food, but he'd leave me alone in the house by myself. He'd come back and stay for a short time and then leave again.

One time, the money he gave me ran out, so I left the house in search of food. I met a boy on the streets of Ghana who introduced me to his family. I helped his mom wash the dishes and I cleaned up for the family. Her name was Kisi. She would cook and give me food because I helped her family. I stayed with her family when my uncle was gone. When he returned to Ghana, he discovered that I wasn't at home. He was very, very upset.

He came to Kisi's house. She was cooking on the stove. My uncle took my right hand and put it in the food, like a spoon, and stirred it in the pot right in front of her. The food was hot.

It burned my hand, but nobody did anything. Nobody stopped him.

My hand was never the same again. It still has scars, even to this day. My uncle said that I brought disgrace to his family for serving other people. He said, "Our family will never work for no one." When I left his house to work for Kisi and her family, it was an insult to him, so that's why he burned my hand. It was because of the shame he felt.

I stayed with my uncle for a little while longer but ended up moving out of his house to stay with Kisi's family again. They were not my blood relatives, but they were the only family I knew.

I stayed with this family for a couple of years. We were given an opportunity as refugees to leave our country and come to America. People from America had come to Africa to hear our story. They wanted to know why we left Liberia. We were all interviewed. If you passed the interview, you were given an opportunity to come to the United States.

So, we practiced for the interview. One day, during our practice, I was replaced by somebody else. The family decided they were not going to bring me to America with them after all. They wanted to sell my place to somebody else instead of giving it to me. The whole family agreed to the idea. To my amazement, one of the daughters told Kisi, "You should not do that." She said, "Johnny has been staying with us for a long time now. He has been serving us. We should take him with us." So that's how I got a chance to come to America with them.

We were truly blessed by the United States Government. They helped us find a place to stay. They gave us food stamps. They put me in school. They gave the family jobs and helped us get familiar with the country. During this time, several people in the family left. They went to different states to find better opportunities. Only four of us were left: Kisi, one of her daughters, her oldest son, and me.

High school was very tough for me. I remember my first day at school. I didn't even know how to get to my class. While I was walking in the hallway, a bunch of guys tried to jump me. I began to have problems at home too. Kisi wasn't giving me any food. Whenever she cooked, she would eat the food herself and then lock the leftovers in her room. She neglected me. But I was a survivor. I figured out a way to open her room to get the food. She felt like I was stealing from her, so she called the police on me. She told them that I broke into the house and took the food. She made up stories about me, telling the police that I was in a gang. She said that I was up to no good and that I threatened her. She didn't want me to live with her anymore. She told me that she was going to send me back to Africa. She met some other African people who helped her come up with a plan for getting rid of me.

During this time, I met a guy named David. He taught a Bible study that I attended and invited me to attend a Christian camp. I told him about the problem that I was having at home. Kisi and I were fighting all the time. Sometimes, she would trick me and ask me to go into a room. She would say she's not going to beat me up, but when I went into the room, she would close the door and hit me with anything she could find: a cooking spoon, shoes, the broom, anything. I asked him to talk to Kisi so that I could have peace with her because she was the only mother I knew. Even to this day, I would still like to stay with her. But it didn't work out. She had her own plan. She wanted to send me back to Africa.

I started getting into trouble. I couldn't concentrate in school because of all the things that were going on in my life. At the same time, I was having problems with gang members in the school. Some of them asked me to join their gang. I told them no, but they kept after me.

One day, while I was in the office at school, a guy had the courage to ask me if I would like to join his gang while we were both waiting to speak to the principal. He wouldn't leave me alone, so I spoke really loudly, "Look, I told you, man, I don't want to get in your gang. I'm in a gang for God." But that didn't stop him from messing with me. So, one day, I found a knife. I put the knife in my pocket and went home. I wore the same pants for school the next day because I didn't have many uniforms. During my PE class, the knife fell out of my pocket. I was suspended from school for a few days and taken to juvenile court.

The school sent my mom to pick me up from the juvenile court, but she didn't want to do it. She wanted me to stay there until she had enough money to send me back to Africa. But God works in mysterious ways. My caseworker was curious about why my mom did not want to bring me home. He sent people to the house several times asking my mom to come get me, but she wouldn't do it. As he began to investigate what was going on, he found out that she was planning to send me back to Africa.

He said to her, "But you came here as a family. Who are you going to send him back to? Why are you sending him back?" She told him that I was not her real son and that I was disrespecting her. We went before a judge to decide the matter. The judge told her that if she sent me back, then everyone else in the family would have to go back as well because according to our story, we came as a family. She did not want to hear that, so she ran away. She left the city. She took all my important documents with her, and I was put into state custody. David became my foster dad for a few years, and then I went to live on my own.

I got involved in drugs and the street life. I was staying in the hood with several different people. My life got really hard. It was empty, and I was lonely. I tried smoking marijuana. Before I knew it, I was drinking hard liquor. I was trying all these things to fill the void that I had in my heart, but nothing brought me peace.

I often stayed with a friend of mine. As a matter of fact, I used to like his sister, so I would go to his house a lot. We all smoked marijuana together. He smoked. His mom smoked. His stepdad smoked.

So one day, he invited me and a few other guys to his house to hang out. He asked us to get some marijuana before we came over. We were going to hang out and listen to music. Music was an important part of my life. I always loved music. I rapped about the things that I saw and about the things that were going on in my life.

After we got the drugs, he wanted to make one more stop. He asked us to stay in the car and wait for him while he went into the house to see his cousin. There were three of us still in the car. I was sitting behind the driver. My friend from Africa was sitting next to me in the back seat. We waited for this guy in the driveway to come and get us. But he never came out of the house.

I saw his cousin coming towards the car. He was a big dude. He opened the back door of the car next to my friend. He took out a pistol and put it on my friend's side and told him to drop off the drugs.

I thought that he was trying to punk us out to see if we were soft. At first, I thought he was just messing with us, but he was for real. He kept saying, "Drop it off. Drop it off. I'm not going to tell you no more." I was terrified. He caught me off guard. Before I knew it, somebody else came and opened my door and put a gun to my head. I reached for the gun and pushed it away from my head. I stepped out of the car still holding onto the gun. I told the man with the gun, "You're not just going to kill me like that." We were both fighting for his pistol. Somehow the gun never went off. But as we were fighting for the gun, he snatched it out of my hand. I fell to the ground right in front of the house. Right in front of the door. I fell with my arms open to the ground. When I fell, I knew I was going to die.

All a sudden, the first thing that came to my attention was Jesus Christ. Now during this time, I wasn't living for God, but I knew of God. I knew about Jesus Christ. I remember crying, asking Jesus to spare my life and to give me a second chance. I told God, "If I have to die today, I'm coming home."

And to my surprise, God spoke to me from heaven. I did not see him, but I heard him. He asked me, "Johnny, where is your home?" God began to question me. God held me accountable. He said, "Johnny, you've been to church. You've heard of me."

The second thing he said to me was, "Johnny, you've been to a Christian camp. They talked about me all the time." God was telling the truth. I went to a Christian camp. The last thing he said was, "Johnny, you have been to Bible study. During Bible study, you talked about heaven and hell. So my question to you is, 'Where is your home?'"

I was speechless. I was terrified. I was crying. I was shaking. Words cannot express how I felt. I never had an encounter with God like that in my whole life. God showed me very clearly that heaven was not my home. When God asked me that question, it was very clear to me that I was not saved. Then he stopped talking to me.

I was still laying on the ground. I could hear people inside the house next to me. They were playing with the door lock. They were trying to open the door, but the door wouldn't open. I laid on the ground for a while. I noticed that I was still alive. I was still breathing. I looked up at the car, but no one was there. Everybody had run away. All four doors of the car were open, and the music was still playing.

I dusted myself off and said, "God, I'm scared. I don't know what to do or where to go. But I need some help. This was not the first time people tried to take my life. Nor the second time.

So many times, you have spared my life. Now I know it was you who spared my life today. I don't know what to do or where to go from here, but I need your help."

One day, I went for a walk by a soccer field in the neighborhood. There was a scripture verse written on the bleachers. It said, "Keep me safe, O God, for in you, I take refuge." I didn't know what the word “refuge” meant, but that scripture became my prayer to God. God led me by His Spirit to His word. So, I meditated on His word. I prayed, "Lord, keep me safe, because in you, I take refuge."

During this time, I was homeless. I had nowhere to go. I used to sleep at other peoples' houses, but I was a problem because of my behavior, so nobody wanted me to stay with them for very long. I was just going from place to place like I did when I was in Africa. Sometimes, I slept outside when I had nowhere else to go.

It was cold one night, and I was sleeping in front of a man's house. He woke me up. He had firefighter clothes on, but they looked like police clothes to me. I looked at him and thought, *What does this guy want with me?* He wasn't waking me up to get me out of his yard. He was waking me up to invite me into his house. He asked me to come in because it was cold outside. So I did. He gave me a blanket and pillow and told me I could sleep in his house. His name was Quentin. He had two other roommates, John and Jeremiah. They invited me to stay with them.

I began to really see the love of God through these men. They didn't know who I was, but they took me in. They risked their life by trusting me. They didn't know what I was capable of doing, but they took me into their house as a stranger. They gave me food to eat and a place to sleep, free of charge.

The other thing I remember during this time was they did not force Jesus on me. They didn't force me to go to church. But they showed me his love. It was weird because I hadn't seen the love of God like this before. In the family that I grew up with, nobody ever showed me the love of God. My whole life I was abused and accused, but these men showed me God's love. I was skeptical of them. Many days I watched them to see if I could understand why they treated me so kindly. What did they want from me? I didn't know if it was real, but they kept showing me God's love.

Eventually, God softened my heart through this community. I remember going to a house church they went to. My heart was still so hard because I had so much anger and frustration in my heart. I really didn't trust anyone, but I went to see what they were saying about Jesus Christ. I wanted to know Jesus for myself. So, this community is where spiritual transformation took place for me. I remember confessing my sins to God, asking Him to forgive me.

I surrendered my life to Jesus Christ and began to read the Bible for myself. I wanted to see what the Bible actually said. I was still asking God, "Why is there so much killing? Why did I have to lose my family?" God began to answer my questions through the Bible.

I saw how God created the world in Genesis chapter one. He created the heavens and the earth, light and darkness, the birds, the fish, the fruit trees, everything. God said, "Now let us create mankind in our image, in our likeness. Let them rule over the fish in the sea and the birds in the sky. Let them rule over everything." And then in chapter 2:15-17, God took the man that he created and put him in the Garden of Eden to work in the garden and to take care of it. God gave him free will. God said he was free to eat from any trees in a garden, except for one particular tree. It was the tree of the knowledge of good and evil.

I discovered from God's word that human beings had disrespected God. They disobeyed him, and sin came into the world. Sin did not just affect Adam and Eve. It affected all people. Through sin, death came to all people. Sickness and hardship were a result of sin—all because men were tricked by the enemy into eating the fruit that God told him not to eat. And we are all reaping the curse of that sin.

As I read the Bible, I started to understand that when God first created this world, He blessed it. He was pleased with it. He had good intentions for it. When I read the story of Adam and Eve's rebellion, I realized how their sin affected me. It was one act of disobedience, but it brought a lot of pain and suffering and wickedness into the world. The rebels in Liberia caused the war because of the sin in their hearts. The guys in my neighborhood who were causing trouble, they had sin in their hearts. And I was guilty too because I sinned against God.

During that time, one verse in the Bible really spoke to me, John 15:16. Jesus was talking to his disciples, but as I read it, I felt like Jesus was talking to me. He said, "I chose you, Johnny. I chose you for a reason, to go and bear fruit." So I accepted Jesus because he accepted me. I was overwhelmed by his love. I said, "God, I'm a sinful man. I'm a wicked man. I deserve death, but you chose to give me life. You chose me for your family. You chose me to honor you with my life. You chose me to go and bear fruit."

So, that is how I came to know Jesus Christ and how he transformed my life. God showed me I wasn't saved. So, I asked him to forgive me for my sin. I asked Jesus to come into my heart and be my Lord and my Savior. In obedience to my faith, I was baptized a few years later. And then I received the gift of the Holy Spirit. Suddenly, God gave me his peace. It was something I never had before, something money couldn't buy. When I say peace, I could walk down the street without fear of people harming me. It was like a burden had been taken off my shoulders.

Jesus began to heal my heart. He began to comfort me in my pain and suffering. So, I love Jesus. I'm glad he did not save me from my sorrows, but he saved me from my sin and from the wrath of God. He died for my sin. My mom and my dad did not die for my sin. They cannot die for my sins. Even my good works are not enough. Only the blood of Jesus that was spilled on the cross of Calvary could pay for the sins of the world.

Now I can say with confidence that heaven is my home, all because of God's grace. Africa is not my home. The hood is not my home. My home is in heaven with Jesus. God in His grace blessed me with a wife and a wonderful daughter. I love this new life. I don't want to go back. I'm glad to have a wife and a family of my own. But most importantly, I'm glad to have a heavenly Father. I'm glad to know that I have a home in heaven where one day, God is going to wipe away all our tears. On that day, there will be no more suffering, no more pain, no more dying, no more sickness, and no more injustice. That is the home where I am going.

Until that day comes, I live to serve God. God chose me to bear fruit for His kingdom, so I worship God with my music, and I help others to worship Him too. I share the good news with others, because Jesus saved me from all my sins. I want others to feel the love that I feel. I want others to find their joy in Jesus.

The Fruit of God's Mission

Johnny's life is similar to our own. Just as God chose Johnny to go and bear fruit for His kingdom, Jesus calls us out of the world into a personal relationship with himself, appointing us to go and bear fruit (John 15:11). Jesus' love empowers us to love others (John 15:9), thereby enabling us to complete the mission we have been given to love one another (John 15:12).

When the church is faithful to love others, Satan's dominion is displaced by God's Kingdom. Those who are in bondage are set free by God's love. We are able to love others because God first loved us (1 John 4:19). Jesus loved us by forgiving our sins

(Ephesians 1:7); therefore, we love others by forgiving them when they sin against us (Col 3:13). Jesus loved us by giving his life for ours (Galatians 1:4); therefore, we love others by giving to them in their time of need (Luke 6:30-31,35-36). Jesus loved us by receiving us into his family even when we were sinners (John 1:12-13); therefore, we love others by extending hospitality to those who experience the brokenness of this world (Isaiah 58:7;1 Peter 4:8-9).

The story of Johnny's salvation is a story of God's love, and it reflects many of the principles discussed throughout this book. Johnny's testimony gives us an example of how God uses the church to advance His Kingdom in the world. Johnny was held captive in Satan's dominion by personal sin, family brokenness, and community violence. God called Johnny out of the world into a personal relationship with Jesus, setting him apart from the world to bear fruit for God's kingdom.

God mobilized His church to storm the gates of Hell on Johnny's behalf. David laid a spiritual foundation in Johnny's life by teaching him the Bible. Although he wasn't fully ready to receive the spiritual truth of God's word at the time, God used the lessons learned through David's Bible study to convince Johnny of his sin and need for a savior during a time of crisis. When Kisi abandoned Johnny, David stepped into the void, providing Johnny with a place to live.

Quentin, John, and Jeremiah served as "restorers of the breach" by giving food and shelter to Johnny when he was homeless. They welcomed Johnny into their home and introduced him to their friends. Johnny became a part of a larger Christian community where he learned more about God's word. The relationships Johnny established through the church eventually led to an employment opportunity as a chaplain at Christ Community Health Services, which is also where Johnny met the woman he would eventually marry.

Although the world might not think much of Johnny as a refugee and an orphan, God saw Johnny as a mighty warrior for His kingdom. God displayed his grace through Johnny's weakness, calling him out of the world and setting Johnny apart for Christian service.

Johnny learned to overcome fear with faith. He believed in the truth of God's scripture and surrendered his life to the Holy Spirit. God gave him a deep and abiding peace. He is no longer afraid to walk the streets of his neighborhood. He regularly shares his testimony of God's grace with the young hustlers he used to run with.

Jesus forgave Johnny of his sins; therefore, Johnny extended forgiveness to Kisi, "the only mother he knew," despite the abuse he received from her as a teenager. Johnny wanted Kisi to experience the same love and forgiveness that he had received. He was not bitter about his past. Receiving God's forgiveness freed him to forgive others. Forgiveness broke the cycle of violence that Johnny had experienced throughout his life.

Johnny continues to live in a community fraught with suffering. He longs for the day when Jesus will bring all suffering to an end. Until that day comes, Johnny is committed to seeking the shalom of his community by bearing fruit for Jesus. He enters into the suffering of others, offering his neighbors the love of Christ. A virtuous cycle of love and forgiveness is being established. The gates of Hell are crumbling. There is hope for Johnny's community.

You Are Commissioned

Johnny is not alone in his effort to bear fruit for God's kingdom. God has chosen you to fulfill His mission, to storm the gates of Hell, by sharing His love with those who are trapped in spiritual bondage.

Remember the three prongs of the sai that were described in the introduction? God has empowered us to share his love with those in need, taking the gospel to the very ends of the earth, for the sake of His glory. I pray that you will put the principles outlined in this book to work.

Start by inviting a few like-minded friends to pray with you. Pray that God's will would be done on earth as it is in heaven. Ask God to give you insights into the needs of your community. As you pray, take notes on the insights God gives to you. Share your insights with members of your church.

As you pray, look for answers to these specific questions. Where are the poor being oppressed by systems of injustice in your city? Who has been ostracized in your community? Who is in need of forgiveness and a fresh start in life? Use the list of ideas generated through prayer to formulate a mission strategy for your church or small group.

Next, pray for the nations in the same way, asking God to show you a specific people group in need of His salvation. Use one of the prayer guides on JoshuaProject.net to pray for people who do not have access to the gospel. Ask God to appoint Christian workers from your church to engage one of these unreached people groups as missionaries. As you pray, Satan will try to distract you with fear and doubt. Use scripture to fight against the enemy. Site specific scripture verses in your prayers that contradict Satan's lies.

Armed with insights from your prayers, convene members of your church or small group to develop a plan for loving your neighbors and sharing the gospel with unreached people groups. Assess the needs of your community. Perform a focus group with a local school, ministry or community group. With members from the community, make a list of all the problems they face on a large whiteboard or sheet of paper. Prioritize the problems by giving each person an opportunity to vote on the greatest need. Ask if there are people in the group who would be willing to partner with your church to solve one of the problems they identify.

You can do something similar with international mission organizations. Frontiers, Pioneers, and the International Mission Board are all organizations that our church has worked with in the past. You can find email addresses for all these organizations on the internet. Ask them about their current need for missionaries. Do they have particular people groups they have prioritized? Ask them for guidance on how to develop a church-wide strategy for engaging unreached people groups with the gospel. Organize a trip to one of the prioritized people groups so your church will have firsthand insight into the fears that need to be overcome with faith to engage the people group with the gospel. As a church, commit to a long-term strategy for reaching that specific people group.

Ask for a copy of your church's budget and assess your church's financial priorities. Does the budget reflect God's priority to the poor and unreached? Is your church's leadership team willing to pray and ask for insight about its giving priorities? Would you be willing to increase your giving if it was directed to the poor and unreached people groups? How will you personally use your financial gifts and spiritual talents to impact the world for Christ?

God is liberating those who are under Satan's oppression. He has chosen you to go and bear fruit for His Kingdom. God has empowered you with his love, for you to love others. You are a living stone, built into a temple for the Holy Spirit. God's Spirit resides in you. I urge you to surrender to the Holy Spirit as you confront the forces of evil that oppose Jesus' reign. Be faithful despite the suffering that will accompany your efforts. Remember that Jesus has already promised our victory, saying, "On this rock, I will build my church and the gates of Hell will not prevail against it." The church has its marching orders. Will you join it on its mission: to the need, to the nations, for the King?

Questions for Reflection

1. How have you experienced the love of God in your life?
2. How will you bear fruit for God's kingdom?
3. Johnny uses a simple model for sharing his faith with others. He answers three questions: What was my life like before I knew Jesus? How did Jesus change my life? What spiritual fruit has resulted from submitting to the Holy Spirit? Share your testimony with a friend or family member, using these three questions as your guide.

BRIDGETOWN

Kim and I started a non-profit organization called Bridgetown to introduce people to Jesus and to lift communities out of poverty. All proceeds from the sale of this book support the work we do through Bridgetown.

If this book was helpful to you, please consider leaving a review on Amazon: amzn.com/B0851SQZ84. Even if it is only a few sentences, it would be a great support for our work. You can learn more about our ministry at bridgetownventures.org.

Made in the USA
Columbia, SC
02 June 2021